ASSUMPTION

Midnight in the City of Springs

JIM DAVIS

unbound CONTENT

Englewood, NJ

ISBN 978-1-936373-35-2
Published in the United States by Unbound Content, LLC, Englewood, NJ.
Cover art: ©2012, Assumption, mixed media, by Jim Davis

ASSUMPTION

First edition 2013

unbound CONTENT

For JDD, SGD, MLD, and ATG

Table of Contents

One.

Two.

Ouroboros

What could be more accurate
than a night owl plunging for mice?
In the lit room beside life
the artist breathes between letters.
Ask yourself, does craft adjust to transmit essence
to the breathless rectangle, or is language
inherently immobile, scribbled with a fist
of ember pulled from stolen fire
on the walls of an empty room? The moon.
The lunacy of its halo set against the city
lights. The artist, commencement
of riotous pre-human sea, beings on the rock
willing to eat themselves to live and breathe.
Alchemy: religion of blind optimism, formally speaking:
Conquering Aeneas, subsumed through hexameter,
consumed by his conquering. Again the page
is torn away, the new page, the bin of torn pages.
The artist, now thick with beard of grime encasing
his jaw and face, wrapped in found rags, resting
in doorways, swaddling infancy.
Frigid cries echo in the city's unblinking cold.
The halo of blue moon, unforgiving—never more
than the night owl
questioning the identity
of anyone willing to listen.
To assume anything other than history repeating
is a sure way to trip over your fortune.
Still, the artist shudders in the doorway,
cradling inception, waking the neighbors
with howls of filthy laughter, raw hands pawing at concrete.

One.

I'm hoping to be astonished tomorrow
by I don't know what.
—Jim Harrison, *In Search of Small Gods*

The stars fell
one by one into his eyes and burnt.
—Frank O'Hara, *Meditations in an Emergency*

ASSUMPTION

Shade

One shivering oak branch
loses an acorn to the soil at the base of an old tree
where a man is napping,
fingers braided atop the great world
of his belly. The only known descendent
of Ricardo Dresden—who
married the daughter of the foremost golf course
designer in South Carolina—who drank himself to death
after the war—they bore a son
who dreams now, only slightly haunted,
that he is sitting in the lobby of a fancy hotel
with a fistful of melting bridge mix, a pocketful of dry mints
and one gold button missing from his coat.
An old woman steps carefully from her car, half drunk
off two fingers of single grain scotch. Heat lines rise
from the line of cars approaching. Dark glasses,
damp collars. Everyone heavy with sweat, especially
the son, who stirs with the impact of an acorn
in the grass. He half opens his eyes, curls further
in his cradle of roots, returns to rest.
Something should be said of the passing clouds
which have never been ignored by a man napping
in the shade of a tree—but he is already out.
Above him, a second oak branch shivers.
Then, they all do.

Fathoms

The sail clapped tight and crooked and spoke,
freeing twenty-eight years of wind from its cheeks.
Back home, the man dug a trench to lay the coal
to roast the pig to feed the village, to pray about rain:
on land, for storm—at sea, for calm. Anyone willing
to lie beside me in the morning is worthy, he said,
and I'm not yet able to use the word *fair* without
bitter ends. Don't make me upset. I am drunk off wine
and watching the sad impressions of standup television.
I laugh with shadows and tide, he said, sending messages
he knew he'd regret. He knows no better than to
catalogue his longing. He writes only because he is
afraid. Surely I'm no good at this, he says. You're not,
said the potted Cat Palm, and don't call me Shirley!
Detached laughter. There are no Titans here, he says, no Gods
to pinch the frill of a Persian rug and pull, to hold me up
against the ceiling fan until I squeal. I used to
dance for kings, he'd say, whistling directions home
from the porter-house; streetlamps flicker out when he's past.
All that he imagines is lost to the open window, the blithe
yellow curtain on the rod. There was a time when there were gods.
He remembers the glimmer of noon on the filet blade
slick with fish, squinting as the boat chugged into berth.
A young woman perched high upon the rail, signaling, Ho!
she signaled, Land ho! And waved her arms, stirring sunlight
and sea mist. Though he was busy digging ditches never filled.
Then the dam broke. And the sail claps explained their absence.

Nearly Risen

Cabinet of concealed nostalgias, oatmeal cookies.
Popcorn kernels ground into the fibers of the rug.
Fruit flies hover like fog. She pulls a box of toasted oats
like a book from a shelf. We walk. We find
some rhythm to begin with. Some beat. Some grind.
The neighbor's beagle paws at the trash. Vile, she said, falling
in love with the advertised sadness. She said
the train smells like effort, sings like angry histories.
She remembers that winter when the blackbird fell, striking
each snow-lined limb of a pin oak. Trembling with cold
soft thuds. On the way, some familiar thumping.
This is a good one, you'll love this, she said,
as we found a seat outside the vegan eatery.
You'll never forget the texture of grilled portobello.
Streetcar tracks suggest that most every preconception is false
given the nature of its projection: inherently uninformed. What God-
forsaken weather might we expect, she asked, tracks flashing
thundercloud heavy, reflected in the dark lens of Foster Grants.
On her phone, sifting through messages and confused, greatly,
by nostalgia, her spring shadow appearing in early August.
She told the story of kittens collected in a burlap sack,
a kid on the bench at the tracks they were thrown to. She's missing
one eye from a childhood accident she isn't quick to speak of. She can
see clearly, but is clumsy through depths of field. Still, he kissed her
on the soft veil of flesh above what's missing. Tender, deep with intention.
She cried hard over the missing kittens. She blew her nose with a quick honk,
barely audible over the shaking of the train. The waiter came with plates
stacked along his inner arm. The eggplant parmesan? That's me, she said. Thanks.
She started talking about pregnant classmates—can you imagine emerging
with the strength to hold your own weight? your own bobbing head?

The Cope Paradigm

A moment in the woodshed with Kathleen—
between the shovels scabbed with dirt, hanging
cultivator claws, chipped clay pots and stacks
of garden mulch—reveals the secret pleasantries
of this life. Among the tongues of hyacinth
getting loose in the garden (once we water them
with pints of rye whiskey and ice), she shakes a glass
of Captain and Coke, close enough to her husband's drink.
stationed in Lisbon, where fried plates of squid and a wedge
of lemon were as big as a crate of azaleas, with a porcelain dish
of basil and oil. So glad, she said, that he'd come back.
Though for a bit of good advice and a buffalo nickel
she'd lead you to the woodshed, sprigs of chickweed
and moss blooming in fists from cracks in the cobblestone
path, slightly buried, the space between stones, engorged
with the musky smell of earth and her unwillingness
to defile Egyptian cotton. But boy, I'll tell ya, a moment
in the woodshed with Kathleen would shake the rust
from the long-handled lopper and the pruning saw—
she'll make you think this whole thing's worth doing,
and worth doing right. And on the darker nights
when weather floods the walk, when throats of the garden
stretch for air, she stays indoors alone, with the window open,
candles dancing on the furniture of empty rooms, dark corners,
a cabinet of medallions, and a green battalion cap—and she,
moaning for a man in a bistro, somewhere, filtering Spanish
through mouthfuls of squid picked in ringlets by a tiny fork,
dipped in a bath of savory oil, collapsing a lemon wedge,

ASSUMPTION

something soulful on the juke box, humming in rhythm,
rattling a glass of cola and ice, a splash of the local rum.

Witch-hunt

A catalogue of sympathies extend from the well-
wishing trials of fire. Touch me, Prometheus, deliver
me this evil. The heat of your life is blinding.
Said *hearth*. Said *stoke* with your poker—you
the great collaborator, you the spark of man
and woman and the science of nonexistence.
Reading Bryson & Bachelard at the window
on the third floor of a used bookstore, scanning
the Flat Iron district. Filtering pages through pigeon
wings, dusting the prison of language. Shouting.
Breaking glass, quick backpedaling bystanders. Why
might it come to this? Why not dig up the garden
of language for bones? Piece them together, end to end,
ball to socket, condyle to fibular tip, then lift the conspicuous
shield of sternum, insert heart, insert a tumbler of rum, an island
of ice. Hear him speak. There are so many bars to be kicked
out of, so little time. Insert some mention of sex.
Adhere to a moral sect, depending on the sex you mentioned.
Though these debonair meanderings will find themselves
realized in ember, sifted through fingers of life, once it has left
the city for a small New England village, a white clapboard cottage
on a hillside, sprawling, stippled with goldenrod, white clover.
Never mind diction, spill the guts of the machine—no one should
speak cynically of progress, they say, of science, they said,
of invented critical nonexistence, sweeping in on the wind,
approaching like the well-intended touch of a god.

Transmigration

On a bus in traffic in the rain, reflecting
on unusable practice, the way that Words
With Friends has limited me to impractical
vocabulary: Qi, Fa, or Ani – the dark, tropical cuckoo,
whose bill can shuck oysters by the bucketful.
On Monday I begin the study of Organizational Analysis
should I decide to show. And in case you were wondering,
I always have Swiss cheese in my Hollywood omelet.
Reader, don't worry, this is going somewhere.
The Germans have a word for ill-fated wander
and it's capitalized, all the time, alive and exuberant
in its Thingness. Like Evanescence in a Dickinson stroll
and Bahnhoff in my haunting dreams: sitting on my suitcase
in the rain, then lost in a rail tunnel outside Munich.
To transfer, transpose, to translate graffiti into a figure
of itself, backwards, basking, reflected, the veritas
of vanity – the vanitas of veins primed to pop
at 3700 feet, pierced by the steeple of the clock tower
stippled with shrapnel of language in a city changed hands.
Prophylactics in the pay-toilet, the WC, and what have we
learned from this? I'll tell you – some non-functional truth
which, as years of morbid solitude confirm, can be crippling.
You say this, yes, and we agree, but then why is it
the flax in this bran muffin, this bitter cup of tea
that breathes of citrus and earth, be so open
as the Frieburg sky in early autumn, as leaves curl
into themselves, brilliantly red, orange, so (despite
their closing, despite the reassignment of gun turrets
as clock towers ticking like a sickle picking gristle from teeth)
so damned inviting – so much, in their passage, amenable? alive?

Patter

The echo of an echo of an echo, uncertain it occurred at all.
Still I stirred, turned to the wall and said, "Come in. Come in already.
I'm awake, quit knocking." Sheets pulled to my chin, nothing. "Who is
there?" I ask. It might have been my father hanging pictures
in the den with a ballpeen hammer, or a man laying rail
the next town over. Attention hung, awaiting a tap; I pulled back
the curtains, light announced itself in a slightly higher pitch.
I remembered one winter near the Alamo when riverboats rocked
and tapped their docks with rhythm of the current. A man from Colombia
Missouri leaned over and said, "The drive from Alabama to Santa Fe is terrible—
nothin' but desert, forgotten earth—but I tell ya, brother, it may seem unbearable,
but the drive from Santa Fe to 'Bama is worse!" The floorboards creaked
as I roamed from room to empty room. I opened slatted closet doors, lifted skirts
to see under the bed. Nothing, still—only an ember of the tapping, the gentle
knocking, the patter trapped in my mind—all but a ghost, a fleck of dust
caught in the light-as-air current of daybreak. The unremitting drum
of water from the tap. Icicles leaking from the gutter—which is alarming
after a night of utter superfluity. The great shoulders of the blizzard slumping,
trickling quickly where a goose set down on the gray lawn, and although
there was a blurred pane between us, I felt the bass of each braking wingstroke
upon approach: the echo of an echo of an action. It's later now, shadows
projected against the buildings are much larger than the substance of which
they are projected—the object near the light is shivering and small
and by the time I arrive at the place where it was born, I am curious
if it ever was there at all. A jazz-man on the corner moans about the devil.
"I am sleeping," I say, "I can't be bothered." The river, back then, was tinted green.
"Texas," said the guy from outside St. Louis, "ain't so big after all—
all they got is big pigs and tall tales." I said to him, "you don't need to see the sun
dipping into the horizon, it's enough to be outside at dusk to understand."
He said, "Yes, but you weren't there when the banana grove caught fire."

ASSUMPTION

"True," I said, but I was lost. I went on hiding for a while, that is, I went on
chasing ghosts and echoes. I grew tired, leaned against cold steel
under the shielding umbrella of a lamppost and I began tapping, tapping.
The song of my tapping echoed to the building tops, through the night fog—
the sun went and came and went again—my hair grew thin and gray.
It rained but I stayed to listen, so pleasantly surprised I could teach it to speak.

Impetus

He stands alone in the kitchen slicing honey apples,
unwraps chestnut leaves from the wheel of Banon
cheese paired with a bottle of Bordeaux. In the cellar
of his country home, a lion paces its cage. He feeds it
chicken bones and frozen pizza. He argues, to roaring
retort, that the lynx is true king of the jungle,
with the hippo not far behind, he is quick
to propose, *the reign of the tyrant is up!* Above
the cage he has hung a three-stone lithograph
of the donkey belonged to Buridan—supposed
to have died of thirst in the presence of water,
hunger, with a sack of oats strapped to his chassis,
though reality, as the print provokes,
is that the ass was torn to bits at tooth-tip,
asserted claw, not unwound by vacillation.
Upon the news of his true death, Jean Buridan,
washing his hands in the river, reflected briefly upon
the small population of Chassey, a commune in the Burgundy
region of France, where three strong men sat at a stone table,
penning the declaration of export: barley, sheep, and poultry
(they keep snails for themselves, pan-seared in garlic
and cream). The impracticality of clean reason
affects the effort of the pastry chef, who discovered chocolate-
chip cookies by mistake, as an earthquake shook shelves
and dropped a dark constellation in sugar-dough. This explains
why, when they are thrown to the lion after thick slabs
of raw meat and hours of political tête-à-tête,
he will sniff a vintage Cabaret, upturn his royal nose.

Poseidon

I refuse to bathe in a world like this.
There are limits here that go unnoticed—
which means that anything is possible; a needle of light
can be blinding. (Was there some mention of detached voices?)
The most gracefully carved of the ocean's beasts,
elegant behemoths in whose mouths children speak
of escape, of bonfire getaways, of every disillusioned old man
who cannot give himself to the task. When my mother was away,
my father made the only meal he knew: chicken dried in a pan
and heaps of white rice with butter and salt. That's all
I remember when she was off on business; that and my dad
perched against the fence when the neighbor boys
got too close to the yard where his children were playing.
Knee-hole blue jeans. Flannel shirtsleeves rolled
to reveal two bulging forearms, stronger when crossed
over his patient chest. The vigilant stare, squinting with each
drag of cigarette. I only needed glimpse, confident
that my sister and I were safe. Such was the repentance
of fallible man, the charge of lots cast toward protection,
to sacrifice, devoted acceptance. Before bed, he asked us
to bow our heads and beg forgiveness, cast off the other life.
Task married to adoration; lone worship. Trapped
in his moustache, the odor of wet tobacco, as he told
the story of Monstro, Pinocchio's allegorical whale
who, should he beach himself, would rest for a moment
in the warmth of the sun, set in the circling shadow of gulls—
how there'd not be time to blink, as the gravity of
this world will crush him like a tomb.

Automatic

It was of course the Douglas Squirrel
trapped in the tangle of furnace
groaning to life with frost.
Everything owns its own light, as though
light were an orb inside an object, emanating
in whisper, then the crack of conflagration—
I said fire; I said it's not a matter
of light-space relating to dark-space, bound only
through geometric fragmentation. (An old man
sits by the hearth smoking a pipe, swirling a tumbler
of small ice.) Order is imposed, the space goes unnamed
by our burning desire to name it. He, teeth clenched
on a corncob stalk, assured me there was no need for language
games—say, speak, inhale experience and exhale
significance. You die without the rhythm of inhale,
exhale—you short-circuit on interpretation—clogged
with ticker tape and gin. (Unholy fingers
rattling keys at the lock.) Oxygen is a byproduct.
Oxygen is witness to a boy with a magnifying glass
frying ants, a girl jumping rope on the sidewalk, under
which exits the sliver of difference
between coda and volta. An old woman lifts the Victrola
needle and sets it, tilts her head like a spaniel. Among the inferno
of agelessness, the fire of the furnace is packed with song,
verse, splitting hairs without unsheathing its clef,
without ever unlocking the woodshed door.

The Way She Shakes

When he returned that night from the sticky floors
of Division street, whiskey weary, he fumbled his keys
in the darkness as the streetlights, mute, were an omen
to the lack of power along the street. Lack of heat.
He kicked off his shoes and found a fresh rot beginning in the fridge.
He sat in the dark, wondered blankly how desire not be
organized by proximity, it seems so much like the least
the universe could do, after cursing him
with dumb sensibilities and lack of sense: an empty pack
of gum like the angel on top of a stack of laundry. A pen cup.
An empty glass stained with wine. He's missed the ingenious
interpretation of misgiving. His irrelevant transportation through days
has fallen into the river, meaning only to test its temperature with a toe.
Cold, he swathed himself in woven blankets, collected on vacation to
San Pedro: pink and faded blue, reminded of ochre sunsets, hidden
by the dark of the room, the moon disguised by clouds
of smoke gathering snow. Too many pickle-backed shots of whiskey.
He heard familiar sounds of lovemaking on the ceiling.
These entangled writhings, wound branches left stranded
in the copper field, at the hour they've been waiting for:
the second gibbous moon this month: hidden, again. The hobos
are dancing on street corners, and Sunday cartoons have illuminated
the depth of their sorrow, the tin can of beans eaten under the bridge.
When the power's out the solution seems simple: paint an escape.
The black train tunnel, impressionist thoroughfare, where,
should anyone try to follow, they'd be flattened by the wall
they've run headfirst into. Some will sense the brief whistle and flash
of oncoming train, be relieved, born again as a version of themselves
and somehow, accordions. He, however, will be permitted
to pass, emerge in the safe harbor of the opposite face,
where, sitting on his own front stoop, he will crack a beer and see

a woman descending steps across the street
in blue jeans and a top just tight enough for history to to hang free
by a chain from her neck, locketed. There will be a dog
leading her with its leash, speaking with its body like a tongue,
of this and every rebirth: spring, and the groan of heat when she moves.

Hollyhocks

Not too, the thousand suns beating.
Stoic irrationality, a habit claimed one winter
on whose flakes the rational no longer adhered.
The man stood serenely on the river bank,
throwing line to the gaps in freshwater skin
fed by hidden streams. Back home, a woman
pinned his clothes to a line. Windswept. The lightest items
near the center of the splintering rope,
where rain fell. A tall tree
stretched across the river, where the dog froze
pointed & barked to a small boat.
The timber in the shed was gathered wet,
sat all summer. The walls are thin, at night, in the wind,
he can see them breathing.
As a boy, he told stories, sang songs around the fire. He bathed
in the ceremony of ramblers. Bobtails pulled apart at the river's edge.
The woman stuck her nose in the air, could smell smoke
on his jacket from nightfires & re-livings.
In the hidden lake, trout move slowly to stay alive.
In the still compartments of water near rocks
slick bodies hide among seaweed stalks
like great silent gods. Should I be
a predator in the muck of leaves and algae, he thought,
while white-bellied trout appear as floating clouds?
The small boat has left us.
The man stands on the bank, noting bubbles between casts, gentle flicks
of demeanor and consequence. The dog barked. Then, the hollyhocks wilted.
And at least one sun split divinely in two.

JIM DAVIS

Reading Time and Listening to Dead Kennedys

Like the rolling tongue and thumping of beetles
at the lamp as Dead Kennedys, drooling over bad brains,
claw their way into an afternoon that has lost itself
to night—misfits evolving into a minor threat, carved
into the arm of a boy in the shower of an old Victorian
home, rolled out before a lawn on the north side of the city—like that.
And something other. Something like a tower in the distance
where a man waves a black flag with the fur of a lion
tied round his shoulders. Strictly polemic. Call guard
and dance with me, whoever you are, to celebrate whatever this is.
Call guard and press seeds into the earth with your finger like the broken
cloud of desertion, absolution, provocation, angst, fight, fight.
Heavy breathing towers. Bricks of hyperbole. Hypertense. Neurocentric.
And then the middle bit, where the town is sacked and the boy's arm
is taken by gangrene, suspicious of ever name he's ever carved.
There is such thing as an early grave. There is such thing as
too much of a supposed but not necessarily good thing.
Somewhere distant, flat stone backs appear in a river.
Incense. Alone in a quiet room. Three logs tucked into a bed
of kindling, wrapped in the sports section, steeping tea.
Consider the pinecone, how it's outlasted tailbones, tonsils,
and every great moment of the twentieth century. And you. Hold your breath.
The struck match of a child on the outside of a pool hall window, looking in.
Halcyon tongue of hyacinth in the hyacinth planter. A graveyard
of stubbed cigarettes. The teardrop flame, dancing, then gone.
The record, were I to have played it, would be skipping now.
Those poor tapping beetles, gray and still, as if an aged version
of beetles, upside down at the base of the lamp, where they seem to be
themselves until you press them, until they crush and fade to dust.

Discovery

Birds on a telephone wire.
Harrowed by blinking lights
in the rearview mirror: gridlock
collecting behind a woman
with smoke escaping the lips
of her convertible hood: the instant
of non-violent congestion: the moment
a car stalls in the center lane
of a crowded highway
as traffic passes: the flash
of history locking horns with the current
of potential. I paddle through afternoons,
stare at the blinking pavement,
sit in silent wonder, marinate
in the wake of the moment:
the inability to describe
how the inability to describe
life elicits beauty through obsession
with accurate naming,
through disenchantment.

Memorial Day

Over the ineffable cellular transmission I've begun
with my father, he tells me of pine trees dripping
in the driveway, so if I intend to come home for barbeque,
park in the sun. It's hot, but there's no other option.
                              I started writing to the girl at the deli
wearing a worn Ordóñez t-shirt. Charming, fit, not far from twenty,
an old English Detroit *D* screen printed on her breast.
                              But I stopped, embarrassed
at the letter she would never see. Read a few essays
in the sun, by a writer I went to school with, who's become
far more successful than I, writing for some
unanimous fair shake.
                              Tic-tacs are passé. A friend has been
turned onto Certs; his friend reminds me that I am certifiably
uninterested in shock-value commentary, crafted semantics
of look-at-me-esteem, bleeding into napkins the morning after.
                              Memorial Day, a fitting tribute:
crimson gore, cerulean snot, tissue paper: crumpling the flag
of counterfeit apathy——one of privilege's many rewards——
and throwing it somewhere not quite, but very near the basket.
                              To be fair, I am skeptical of anyone drinking Pepsi,
or Coke for that matter, and I am thoroughly unconvinced
at my reasoning.
                              The Californian sandwich I eat is warm before it's done.
90 degrees today, at least. Shadows teasing right angles from crates
of planted daisies and snapdragons, tilting in the heavy heat.
The song on the radio says, *I'll start this off without any words* …
                              … and I remember that there is no God-forsaken metaphor
for memorial. Only memory. Only praise. An aphid crawling over my wrist
on a Monday, free of work, contemplating the metaphysics of war,

ASSUMPTION

the practicalities of overpopulation, considering whether
or not to tip thimbles of tequila, unchased, until they burn with sick
forgetfulness, and I fall asleep in the garden, wake to the breath of a hose.
Interstate 90's mostly free.
Debate with me the batting average of every major leaguer
in the Midwest. Say the names of fifteen minors, and then I will
believe you. The neighbor says most people don't have faith in in politics,
which means they're unable to wrap their minds around the possibility
that what's projected can be plucked and collected in the wicker basket
of the system. Soured by cat calls of the underrepresented, or otherwise
uninformed.
Brother, there's only one way
to cook a brat: boil it in German beer, then sear the skin of it
on a fresh, hot flame. Yellow mustard. Gasoline. Raw onion. Beans
on the side. That's the way my father woulda done it, he says,
remembering the mother of his high school buddy, how they folded
the flag and handed it to her.
How the horns were held to their heads.
How she rocked and shook and couldn't breathe.

Glaring

I just want to observe you, if you have heard something
Of Alaskan salmon, specifically their mating habits,
Please darling, fill me in!
There's a right way to do this, and a wrong one.
That sent her off, and with this note I give her up
Once and for all. Although, she quivers
As I come up behind her to kiss her neck.
She says, I have never been
So happy. So lost and forgotten
Go socks and mittens. Spoons and forks
With the unfaithful moon, no doubt, who
Casts himself in that pale blue hypocritical light
He casts on us and gutters alike. Do not spoil the salmon
With the heartbreaking way they were made. Lie to me,
If you have to, just don't spell conjectures
With your finger in the fog, don't tell me of the moon
Whose fists are poised where your pretty face might once have been.

Lunch at What Was Once the Depot

A small bird lands in the brush near the street
after my chicken sandwich arrives and he will not
stop talking to me. Pesto, ciabatta, distracting
clicks and whistles and rustling of leaves. A fly
rubs its hand together, risking its life at the edge
of the spout, where a spot of heavy cream turns
into a small porcelain ewer. There are rules
to language. Ewer seems far too effluent to be
a place for milk. There are rules to the brain and
its placement, its organization of things: Spanish
and English, for example, are stored separately.
I am clicking the back of a pen and tapping it
against my teeth, constantly distracted by the tiny
bird making racket in the brush near the street.
Surly, I return to my studies when a man
in a camouflage cap asks directions to the train.
What I tell him is mostly accurate. You are almost
there, I say, take a left at the stone staircase, go down,
you'll see a plaque announcing the 1996 landing
or passing of the Olympic torch, churning through
town to Atlanta. Already they are stringing lights
through the trees. It's hard to be nostalgic when
you are never far from home. Grounded, unmoved—
see also: stagnant, unused. There is no possibility
without risk. The post of every bike rack is shackled
to a bike—that is, grounded to the mobile part
of said equation. Three pigeons on the tinstone
station ledge, and already I am worried
that *equation* was the wrong word. But it's too late.
The waiter in the Reebok t-shirt has returned

JIM DAVIS

with the bill, and I still have to be at work. To think
that another in the same situation might carve
his name, or near directions, in unrecognizable script
or dip his fingers into a sweet light coffee to stir
the cream and save the fly and slowly sip what's left
past staining teeth and souring tongue, close his eyes
and breathe the subtleties of therapeutic rewiring, muted
wail of a train, wherein whose wake he once set down
some Swedish fish, a plastic comb, his first handful of coins.

Freight Horn

His right ring knuckle was aching, it would rain
soon enough. Happiness will tip the balance
of broken Sundays and profitable Tuesday afternoons—
sleep and sunlight, sunlight and wakelessness, in the wake
of an insomniac? not he—it is the night
that cannot rest, continues to prod his dreams
with breeze filtered through a screen his father replaced
after he punched a hole through it, to get in; it is night
shuffling leaves of the walk, that silent motion
stirring the neighbor's dog to speak. Inspire me, she says.
He reached for a pad of graphing paper at the bed table
where his glasses sat, half-folded, where he outlines
the logistical interface of aperture in sky, those stars, these burned
up robes—they free, they out, or not, or neither, either way
its indecipherable by morning, still hours away. He shakes
doves from knotted branches with his babble: I would say
that, that just don't let me … go dancing, I say … she said
the boy riding koi in the center of the fountain, spitting
mist into the night, he said he'd share the secret dark
if I stole a rib from the parlor—would you like me
to tell you how wrong that is? I would have to pull apart
the chest of a heaving man—a pig at least—the beating heart
of all the bloodshot nonbelievers! I would take you
to the ridge of a hill, like slicing white elephants, a train
splitting them with air. Ernest, are you there? she says
to the empty stacks of luggage on the page.
I'm sorry dear, I'm back now. How long was I out?
he asked as the train's mouth stirred a rain cloud from sleep.

Tavernous

His heart slugged as the sun sank.
Poisons of the world, she suggested
from the back seat of a burgundy van.
Out of work carpet salesmen
watch daytime TV until it is acceptable
to saunter down the road for drinks
where Baker & Wild Bill hang out,
where the rubber mats behind the bar seem unable
to slough their smell, no matter
how many times they're run through the wash.
Desperate, they drink away the final hours
of prospect. A familiar plight, the premise
of countless Sunday conversations
between women in bonnets eating horseradish sandwiches
at the lip of the Rotary garden, flicking coins
into the stream of a pissing cherub,
spitting back mist. At the tavern,
stubbed cigarettes like nightcrawlers
in a graveyard of ash. Blue fluorescence
from beer promotion: a woman pouring water
from a jug, a mountain stream, a firedog
& thundering horses. Smoke Outside,
the sign reads, faded & forgotten.
A shaking arm rattles in the jukebox,
reaches into a catalogue of scratched records
for Knights Bridge, Life is but a Dream,
something to encourage the tapping
of toes on chrome pipe, shuffling loafers,
a subtle sway, perhaps, of hip & mind.
These new days, behind us, their sharp
features cut with blue awning light.

About Bill

He should be coming at you with a straw hat.
If you don't see him, I soon will. He wonder
if I've met the girl I'll marry or the man I'll kill. My father
planting snapdragons in the garden, hanging tomatoes
cast shadows like squid: squid in the briar, squid in an orchard picking apples.
He split the soil fed with pig shit with a hand like the strong face
of a shovel: a digging spade, a sheltering trowel,
to bury fists of bulbs and teardrop seeds. Please, he buried
the bit of finger taken then released by the snout of a hog, pouring slop
in a Galesburg hog-house, one slow summer
when his grandfather, Olmstead, set the dandelion seed to air, to breathe
fire across the prairies of wester Illinois, when he, the bringer of ghost bulbs
was still butchering hogs. Cousin Bill fell in a well
on his way home from haystacking, with a pitchfork like a lance, a straw hat.
He was thinking about the dark-haired girl in class, lectured
on the delicacies of writing curriculum, stealing glances,
watching her laugh. He wonders if she has seen anything like his father,
torn to bits by a coyote pack, in the garden, planting snapdragons
in this, our suspicious and curious earth.

Exhaust

Sunday morning, I spit thick into the sink.
A carpet of haiga on the hardwood floor: drawing paper
and india ink, instinctual strokes, a red solo cup
stained purple at the rim. There is no Zen
like staying up late, waiting for inspiration
to settle. Ornamental skull, forgive me: *Dia de los*
locos. En las bocas de los lobos. It might be too cold to sit outside,
too dark and hungry, so I'll bring a coat, and a Spanish translation guide,
and the cape of a water buffalo, folded in a canvas sack, beside aloe
vera exclamations, bent bristles of a collapsed toothbrush,
a hard green bar of soap wrapped in paper towel, a whinstone
flint and fire. If one were to be paid for the struggle and dilemma
of feeling pity for the pitiful and all its subsequent guilt,
I'd be a regular six-figure shmuck without a flickering idea
what it's like to be divided. Benjamin Rush split the brain in two
hemispheres and said *choose*. Sitting with a cranberry pecan muffin
and coffee at the corner of Milwaukee and Evergreen, I see him running
to catch the bus, the 56 north at 3:13, a sack of axes and smelling salts
rattling in his hand, churning air with his other to propel himself,
chugging, churning, hustling, as if turning cream to butter,
a man to something other than pasted smithereens.
No, I said, spitting cranberry seeds into potted sunflowers,
bobbing atop thick, bristly stems, not even close, I said, peeling pieces
of paper from the hard bar of soap. Shook my head. But what, I said
could you possibly have hoped for? Most people have a place to be
and teeter, instead, on the brink of attention, spilling plasma,
stoning the terror of an afternoon, coughing its exhaust and smiling.

ASSUMPTION

Church Outside of Pittsburgh

On the morning of the new year, the volunteer
rectors are sworn in. There's protest, there will always be
as New Year's day is the hangover holiday, and the pews
are nearly empty. The smell of dust is overwhelming
and every shift of weight creaks through the chapel, echoes
off the vaulted ceiling, through chandeliers hung over
the meager congregation, and into her upturned palms
as the chorus begins: choir of steel men,
wives of steel men, and children born of solder
filling a mold. Most everyone dressed
in going out clothes: khaki pants, pressed, suit coats
and collars. She will take these disturbances,
press them together, rub her hands until sin is a paste,
cleaning from them the labor of the day, previous indiscretion
from the newly initiated. He, with a three day beard, two pews
back with dark streaks across his face, set his cap
on the bench beside him. What was stolen
has been sold, what's reaped is sowed and he cannot
sit through a sermon without thinking of sex. No, he said
to himself in the presence of the Lord, no. Do not
lay it all out there, you know how this goes.
Some things must linger close to the chest.
He flinches as the robe of the crucified savior danced
in the light of many candles. He scratches himself
at the scalloped neck of a limp collar, hides his dirt-nails
in a hymn book. Peace be with you, he murmurs,
conscious of his callous hands, shaking reticence.
And with you. Rites, rituals, phallic symbols
contain him, keep him coming back to that same pew.
He played Santa at his girlfriend's Christmas party, he fit

the suit and now attempts to stifle a belch in his fist.
It's not right to lust when you're expected to worship.
The belch came as the organ hummed to life, no one heard,
but it smells like shellfish and malt liquor, apples
and it sends a twenty something man in a hooded sweatshirt
out the cathedral door and into the alley, where he is pleased
by unseasonable warmth, the glory of another beginning,
doubled over in the alley, coloring snow with the night prior.
Back inside, Lady Verdant leans across the aisle collecting alms,
testing the limits of a burgundy sweater.
What shame, it seems, he said, taking out a dollar
and slipping it into the basket, to delight in your curse.

Correspond

A woman walks into a bank – stop me
if you've heard this one – she lost her left hand
in a boating accident, a weekend at the cottage
of the family of her boyfriend who left her
for a pharmacist, some guy with a condo outside
Atlanta, with fantastic penmanship. She has this
on strong authority: a friend from Cornell University
whom she shared the choir with, bonding
through crescendos and innuendos over wine.
Is it true, listening to Mozart makes you smarter?
One of them shouted, turning the stereo knob
until nachtmusik rang in their ears, already ringing
from Riesling – they'd try anything to cure disorder.
She's filling out deposit slips, over and over
when a man walks into the bank – you have to see
where this is going – and drags his feet over the mat,
spreading salt from the walk. He unzips his coat, unwinds
his scarf. She keeps writing. He says hello, benignly
but she keeps on writing. Fifteen thousand three,
thirty eight hundred sixteen. Stripping complication, she
hums the song of the forgotten. These are the roots
of the pullulate. These are the rules. Bodies stir
and echo after. Outside, in the cold, some hum, some snarl,
some cry, bleat, and whimper. Small eyes begin to flicker.
Every candle should match the candle of its company,
we ought synchronize their lighting and delight not
in a similar smolder, but in the small chaos of flame,
the subtle scripture in dripping rivulets of wax. After
filling out slips for impossible deposits, she stows them
under her bed, in a shoebox next to her letters from God.

Bunker

What demands might we,
that you would surrender the hill?
This is why I say everything I've said: for you
the sky would lie down in a puddle of effluence
and gasoline, paint rainbows. Fight. Pistols fell in winter,
and the old man was eaten by hogs in the hog house.
There is no need to take the hay bales from under
denim scarecrows grinning dumbly at harvest-dusk,
they will be there in the new year, I have it on good
providence. A child raises her hand—What's the difference
between effluence and influenza? Better yet,
what's the question? What's the worst thing
you can imagine, in regards to drinking blood
from a steer, is it tonguing clots from a spoon?
What's the dumbest thing you ever had to do
for acceptance? Say I love you? Say the sky fell?
Say the same damn thing over and over for sake
of claiming an already obsessed horizon. It's noon,
and the sun is not rising, rain instead has risen.
Say again, with a mouthful of seed,
what's the difference between hiding and being hidden?
What devils might we, desperate hill,
once it's you we have claimed? Might we be forgiven?

ASSUMPTION

Boca Grande

Beware the odor of boats touching, shrimp ferries
churning the harbor with a slow custard gurgle. Two grubby
anglers in flaccid caps wait for catfish, cast, wait and cast.
Prone to trivia, she carved the briny air: *Did you know*
that Lincoln made his own soap? She said before
he was licensed in law he was a licensed barkeep, shaving ice,
scrubbing glasses with a towel over his shoulder, listening
to the terror of the American workday. She has labored
to follow in his footsteps, though when she says she makes soap
she means she presses small islands of old soap together
so they stick. Gulls swarm the bait discarded by catfishermen.
Time has a grip on all things, we can only hope
for patience, she said, and then, *where are we? why would we*
stand in line – what are we waiting for? Juice, said the man
beside her, it's the juice—weeping cells of orange pressed
with a hint of lime—a citrus dance, he said, if your mouth can
handle it, like standing at the spot of the differing citrus
handshake, interlocking branches, where they shiver and drip
in the rain—stand here, or stand there in a storm with your eyes closed,
mouth open and skyward, to drink the zest of planted commingling—that,
and rum. She didn't recognize him, although they seemed
to be enwreathed in familiar fog. And of course, my dear,
this light exaggerates your eyes. She pinched a smile as a thin
wind picked up. She tipped sunglasses to the end of her nose,
glaring suspiciously over bone-white frames. *You will indulge me,*
she insisted. Once inside, they drank together. He kept staring
out the window, recanting travels, unwrapping the knife
he smuggled through the border—a blunt blade to spread butter
with a pearl handle, fastened with copper to copper. *Oh my,*
she said. She shook her head, replaced her shades, which she had

fixed in her pulled back and nearly platinum hair. *You'll do*
anything to get out of doing dishes. Remember that summer
when new beauty could drown the odor of rotting fish
and gasoline? *I do,* she says, collecting plates and stacking glasses.
She opens the screen with her shoe, lets the dog out and goes in.
He leans back in his patio chair, the highway reminding him
of the whiz of boats freed from harbor shallows, thick willow reeds.
Wind shakes the branches where the lime tree meets orange.
He shuts his eyes: birds, chimes, blunt fists of dropping fruit.

Potential

Today is alone with itself in the kitchen.
Any winged thing should be able to fly,
set down in a safer arrangement, one in which
the hollow feeling is less. Touching
pots and pans, something dropped. Steam
from trembling lids. Some plucked thing turning white.
Booth after empty booth, chairs turned up on tables
like legs of upturned bugs, dead of something
other than the hard sole of a loafer. What fare?
What the bean is there to do? Inexhaustibly inefficient
he asked for aubergine on his artichoke sandwich—more
organs, he said, if you please. A couple at the register
haggling the check. He climbed to the roof, another booth
left empty. Subsequent rungs ring of numb subsequence.
Man, he decided, drinking in the foul city view,
it sure is lonely up here. He shut his eyes,
scents and sounds insisting dreams are real. There is pleasure
in knowing that they will come and there is something left to do.

When Everything in the World Was Wet

It began in the usual fashion, a small toothache
in my right rear molar. Smell of brewing coffee
after a good hard sleep, how rare it has become
to wake refreshed. The day was announcing itself
as something to note. I sat on the patio, that morning,
considering the starlike shells of huckleberry seeds
dropping into short grass and clippings, with a sound
like a television muting. The coffee was terribly hot
and burned and made my molar ache, but I sat
with my hands around it, warm. Pen and pad splayed
open on my lap. Nearby, rows of gray baby rabbits—
dead, stacked neatly, facing the same blank direction. Light rain.
Which reminded me of the dream I had the night before,
eating in a greasy spoon, pigeon cooing as bells
announced entry, a young boy playing clarinet
in the corner booth. The waitress brought me a plate
of scrambled eggs, spilled some on the way, picked up
what she could manage with long French tips, kicked the other
spongy fragments under the neighboring table. I'll eat those eggs
I said, but you'll have to do something about those shoes!
(Roman rope sandals laced up her calf, tan and toned.)
Someone attached a doorknob to the trunk of a tree, which was fine.
(And appropriate, given my affinity for rabbit holes.)
The waitress returned with a paper sack of apple cores, folded over,
asked me to leave. Now I'm back to the image of, as I slept,
a mother rabbit mournfully stacking leverets, lit only
by a scornful moon. What worship? What effluence is left
for such a task? Which days are best for scheduling
an appointment with the dentist? I wish to God I had a hammock
to sway myself to sleep. I wish to God I had a name not given me
by the enlightened chatter of jays. Tomatoes were clawing at their vines.

ASSUMPTION

Two squinting eyes above the fence. What rest, I said, what kindly rest.
Mud packed in streaks beneath my fingernails, smeared to the quick.
Flood, said the crane, flying tight above the scene and understanding,
casting pall and shadow on the patio where I write. Flood, he said,
landing softly in the marsh of moons forgotten, and never-ending night.
Two squinting eyes above the fence. What rest, I said, what kindly rest.
Mud packed in streaks beneath my fingernails, smeared to the quick.
Flood, said the crane, flying tight above the scene and understanding,
casting pall and shadow on the patio where I write. Flood, he said,
landing softly in the marsh of moons forgotten, and never-ending night.

Crisis: Chrysanthemum

Sitting kitty-corner to the Zen Liquors store, he worried
he was too much like his father to enjoy himself.
Taxis hailed and boarded. He knew better
than to leave the lights on, or play Vivaldi at improper octaves
which depended on the day, relative to rent, divided by time
spent at the tavern on the corner. The woman across the way
was looking for someone well read, whose abstract language
left him stranded in a crossword existence, where
the abstraction of others kept him at a distance, fed
the uncertainties he became. Not after whiskey-sick
coated his lapel, or his inheritance fell unsounding
into his well of debt—only when he felt the texture
of her mouth, velvet ripples like a sand bank, did he ever
see the world for what it was. 50 is the new 40, he said.
And since 40 is the new 32, we're in fantastic company, he said.
Ah, to be young again! He decided now, and since, that he would
kill his father. A new light shone upon the slow walk home
past the steel mill, one he had grown used to, but never
accustomed, depending of course on the day's color. A closing
remark, something well beyond beauty or pleasure, or disruption.
Touched on the wrist by his lover, he shook himself out of Zen
Liquors and returned to the day, where she and he walked slowly back.
Honeybees tracing perennial paths to mum-buds.
Stopping now and then to cup the jonquils.
Making subtle changes to the ledger.

Winnetka Warrior Reflects on Prior Fall

Find him brimming with obsession
as a plastic super hero melts and blackens.
Thick heat, slow fanning of a stage door.
When you say beatitude, he says the good old days.
When you say quiet remembrance, he admits nothing
and turns again toward the fire. What's new?
The holidays have changed, for one.
He dropped his pack first, let his legs dangle,
shoved off the ledge and landed, hatched
the window shut behind him. Roaming the bushes
in a hockey mask, living in the sound of exhalation
like the movies, he thought, stalking soccer players
from the cover of wilting shrubs. All afternoon he snuck,
dug holes for burying, found thing to bury. A ball
rolled out of bounds to his cover, so he ran out, kicked it
in the wrong direction, ran back. He'd been promised a monster
movie, and bags of candy, instead here's this dug hole
behind a willow he used as a toilet. He zipped quickly, bees
lifting from broken ketchup packets to investigate. Mud-caked
fingernails, twigs woven through bramble hair. Can we leave now
please? You're trying too hard to remember, he said, there has to be
a symbol to build upon. This isn't it. He felt guilty for generations
lost to war. He knew that much. It's time to go, he thought, and grew
restless. Years spent there in the bushes. Heal the World played
from the cassette deck as they drove home, too tired
for anything. The staircase covered in brown shag carpet
became a runway, after a nap, for the plastic laundry hamper he rode.
He remembers the first window he broke, with a snowball

thrown at his sister that winter. He was so happy
to have it over with. What a struggle it was to walk around knowing
the day would come when your mistake would break a window.
Decided the next time he went to watch a soccer game and a ball rolled
over to his position, he'd charge and kick it, he supposed, all the way
to the moon. He word a mask and ate so much candy he puked green and
blue. He knew that kids were always almost out of their minds.

Whinny

When she left she saw the skyline had been drinking.
A rusty paint bucket props the door and she forgives,
so easily, the winter. It's warm. The sixty-three year-old
Mississippian chased down the Hungarian refugee
who snatched her purse. She struck a cigarette to calm
her heaving chest. A boy rocks back and forth on a coin-horse.
She stocks up on paper kitchenware and towels, thinks back
to Aberdeen and owls questioning the night, wonders
if there's method to the madness of swamp-singing—
hysterical hissing, the chirps and ready-when-you-are bellows
from bullfrogs the size of catcher's mitts. She treats herself
to a cup of soup, spoons tomato, ginger, black sesame
from a paper bowl, sips cappuccino on a bench
outside the museum. The boy from the sprung horse straddles
the see mechanism, then saws, shifts weight. He shoves
a handful of rocks in his pocket, haggling equilibrium.
The bus pulls in, she gets on; it goes, she gets off.
Home, she sees that silence has coiled itself in an empty space,
a cobra wound in a wicker basket, sealed in a mason jar
with a cotton ball of perseverance. Preservation is not a word
for the sane. She pens a few letters and climbs the black fire
escape to the roof, where ventilating pipes point, break and curl.
Night, and the blinking stars like sinking buildings, reaches
of an earth to which she once belonged. She's aware
of what another beginning might look like.
She sets her purse down and covers it with newspaper,
gathers her skirt and leaps straight up into the air,
knowing full well the gravity here could never hold her.
By the time she returns, the buildings have collapsed.
Time, she says, is a dimension for the usuals. On landing,
she pulls only what she needs from the rubble
and hangs on tight, knuckles turning white on the reigns.

The Boat We Rode in on Sank

and my arm fell asleep beneath your neck. Rocking
steady at the precipice of great falls, gently, you wept.

We gathered what we could find and turn quickly into
kindling. A knife loping sprigs of green from logs.

The auspice of great cranes which fell and became
craters, or cupholders, depending on what you prefer

to gain. Another beer? Sure. Let's make this interesting.
Let's be in our right minds when we bring ourselves back

to the soil, upturned with broken-bottle spades, graves
crowned with bottlecaps. Do you believe the whispering

of dual-turbine engines? The 4:15 to Cleveland is low enough,
it seems, to touch. Which means we have rediscovered

at least a hint of path, or pathos: the old dirt road, carved
into the beach of rust and worry, eaten in meters

by the over-indulging ocean—the spirited, fatherless sea
losing itself to itself through a fury of buckets, flotsam

foaming in deference to the auspice of stars it reflects.
Lit by firelight, she folded her everloving arms and said

If it came down to it, darling, I'd cook and eat you, I promise.

Black Dress

Early winter mist. Walking through a different hour,
collar pulled tight to my jaw. I find, taped to the trunk
of a sidewalk tree, erect in its grate, a quivering notice,
damp: Lost Black Dress, it says, in long Calibri, the most
desperate font—beneath, a recount of the occasion of its loss.
A birthday party cracks a bottle of champagne and the popper
puts his mouth to the foam. Pierce & Wood, where at the back
end of one hot summer night two old friends stood, half-drunk,
shifting weight and talking. Three separate collections of wind
chime hung from the eave of the Victorian on the corner. You have
never heard anything like Jeff Buckley, he assured. He stayed up late
playing guitar, combining chords and hoping for something close to
Lover, You Should Have Come Over. He saw the sun rise, poured a glass
of water and went to sleep. When he woke the world was dry, his eyes
crusted over, the dog tied to the fence was tugging at its leash.
Blizzard. He put the dog down. She has gone to Carolina
to open a stone-oven bakery. A friend of a friend jumped
from the chimney tower at the textile plant. One summer they threw
tiles from that same roof, watched them pop and smoke below,
the white dust of crash speckling blacktop, an earthly satire
of night sky. Over coffee one afternoon, she said, You die
when you land, so long as you're not attacked by your own heart.
After all, it wasn't the jump that killed him. Don't fear the jump.
(The neighbor boy was hiding in an oak tree, picking eggs from a nest.)
They embraced and said goodbye. Wind chimes touched each other,
themselves. Her train pulled into Chattanooga near dark.
When the bakery burned down she moved back home, but never spoke.
He poured himself a glass of milk and closed the door to his bedroom.
He read from *The Art of Extended Haiku*, folded his glasses on the bureau.
When he shut the lights off a dog barked. He could not help

but picture her naked, walking home in the rain. He knew, somehow
that nothing would ever be the same. Guilt crept over him like fog,
like smoke. There comes a time in one's life when you have to admit
the fire won't quit and it's time to call upon the hose, smother the embers,
crack a window. When the wind blew limbs of a baron oak against the screen,
the street lamp cast itself black upon a dress, curled like a lion in the street.

ASSUMPTION

Beating Pacific

Beheading saintdom, so goes the plot of those pining hours:
night, creeping like mice along pantry baseboards. Climb upon the
unencumbered platform, raw slices of fresh canvas, unafraid

of the void, covered with the color of evening, pressing
the level weave of gesso'd fabric. In somber hill country,
constellations like Cepheus, Draco, Ponce de León, &

a surprising delivery of Salt Peanuts by Dizzie
Gillespie, Charlie Parker & three other horn blowers
that no one could name. Original light begins the same, with-

in an object, then without, spread over the known world like our
immediate terror, lost in a crowd. In a sea of hands
& hips, hairy, vascular calves, or blue jeans with unidentifiable

script of their seams, the forgotten child will grab the closest hand—
lost only upon the realization that the hand he holds
is as foreign as the hard rib of an eel hidden in the dinner he will eat

years later, sitting on the lip of a fountain near the site
of the housing market crash. White mist. He thinks if he ever saw
a pineapple tree, how hard he would shake it. My God, he sighs,

I'd ring its trunk & catch the breathless fruit in its fall. What night,
he insists, beating the Pacific with his fist, holding tight
to the girl of his dreams: what star-lit, jug-wine, bell-struck night.

JIM DAVIS

Bad Boy

after Eric Fischl

The young man can't afford the story
the way the old man tells it. There is
something suggestive in the art of
burning books: some theft, some wound to be
tongued and tested. The light drooling through
the blinds in thick strokes is barring, unsighted:
angled smoke, soft geometry.
Adolescent stigmata, dusk, the musk
of darknesses we suggest. The space beneath
the floating bed is the purse is the crease
of two walls meeting, the union of fruit
in a bowl. How far are you willing to go?
Will you stroke his parted hair? Plunge into
the distance between pillows? Shallow-
chested colonel's son. Blue walls, want for
cherubim. This space, where the veriest
fold is ripe. This bed, whose wanton spread
cannot help pleating.

Back to the Beginning

Every now and then he remembers the way
bison peppered slow hills, the iron imprint
of hot metal in flesh, a scorched iron
on carpet, the small underground bathroom
where he was trapped for days by a spider
on its haunches, risen and gnashing. A pattern
of sun through lace. Iron smell of cellar.
Touching an empty casket. He remembers
when spiders were men and squirrels
were girls. Running along the thoroughfare
where trapped wind whistled, the illusion
of speed. Joanne, migrant from Kilkenny, ran rhubarb
through the neighbor kids, wore orange lipstick,
told his six-year-old sister the truth
about St. Nick. He cried when the Easter Bunny died.
The crucifixion held his attention
as long as it took the Shaman to pull the heart
from his sacrifice in the Temple of Doom.
He knows exactly how many cards one can flick
into a ten-gallon hat, can measure that in pistols,
divided by pints of beer. (One night, the barrel waivered,
he steadied the notch on a mason jar and shot.) Later,
he stumbled upon Goya painting Saturn, with one arm
hanging like a limb from a hillside cavern.
He saw the beach white with sun from the window.
After the gunfire, Goya was no longer able to hear
Napoleon's army storming Spain. A fine sort of quiet.
Everyone was stout under the weight of faith they felt they had
wasted, after the earth quaked Lisbon to its knees.

JIM DAVIS

Malbec, mussels, Egyptian squid he finds unsavory
after many seasons far from home. He remembers
a dream, running along the thoroughfare with a herd
of bison thundering behind. He returned home to find them
toppling the monument, tracing their names in dust
with fingertips, bent on hands and knees.
Then, with sirens, they rise and gnash, rise and gnash their teeth
to bleeding stumps. Blue and red. Unfamiliar thunder.

He remembers his first switchblade, how he bled
when all he wanted was to carve his name.

Awake From Disquiet

He went on listening to oak branches
drag leafless fingers across the shingles of a slanted roof
like a doe nudging a still fawn, limp
and visceral—pleasantries of the world
be damned. Don't worry, she said, there's still time …
Still time, as if seconds echoed in death, a cadence
for never having been: measured nonexistence. [*learn quickly*,
she said, after waking from a sweat-soaked dream of herself
dividing the forest in the skin of a bear, *to listen to yourself*]
She sleeps. He goes on, in deference
to her dreaming, rises slow and quiet, tiptoes
to the kitchen. The fridge lamp blunts the room,
lights him from below like a Bordeaux dancer, a figure
from la Belle Époque, fixed in the grip of Renoir, Lautrec
or some other drunk slurring encouragement at the Moulin Rouge
with an off-white finger of pastel. His neighbors were
on holiday in Taos, he could see through the crystals
spreading over the window like a web, an array of newspaper
collecting on the stoop. He'd save them in the morning.
He grabbed the neck of a beer and held it, tilted
against the lip of the countertop to crack it open. The door shut
with a gasp. And he, remembering dreams, opted for the teeth
on the end of a corkscrew instead. He sketched a face in his breath
on the glass, touched the bottle to his lips. He drew the curtain
to dull the sound of crying from the forest
which, he decided, was not *crying* so much, but the sound of sad
confusion, the way a doe must cry: some haunting, unnamable quiet.

Hoverflies

A furious stink of fog above
the soldiered collection of pigeons
perched on the fountain ledge.

The soul of the city tucks its face
into its dusty feathers, jumbled smells
of sewer and barn, garbled in arrogant cooing.
Portia, smoking cigarettes in the garden apartment

hair some silver shade of lilac, she refers to them
as flying rats. These bobbing foragers, some
so pasted with grime their feathers turn up
like a post-punk hairstyle, unashamedly filthy

and casual. A man on the corner teaches his son
the proper way to fold a handkerchief, waiting
for the bus. On this block, there are fluctuating stages
of assimilation. In the park, some city pigeons

are wounded – one flies crooked, broken wing,
while another is missing a scaled stretch of talon
bound at the stump of ankle by a rusted length
of barbed wire. There is no denying them

scavenger hordes, picking the city of filth,
soiling a filthy city. All said, we must not abandon
the aforementioned soul, timid and soft: city dove
properly anxious in a crowd. Alone at the lip

ASSUMPTION

of a puddle, safely distancing herself from the fountain-
sentries, nodding and cooing in superfluity.
She bobs, little dove, letting her gentle beak slide
demurely into the puddle, cooing essential lament.

Like the soft blonde florets of climbing ivy, she lingers
in a buzz of hoverflies, tucked into a shadow:
wallflower, waiting to be screwed into pigeonhood.

As It Pertains

Who has not spent an afternoon considering
whale evolution? How many nights can you lie
awake, hoping Stevie Wonder's harmonica will sing
you to sleep? Someone in the audience is whispering
in a nonthreatening way, he might be the leader
of these free United States—imagine that, then see it
on Channel 13 (the number we once feared, then worshiped,
loathed, grew to appreciate through re-appropriation:
the amendment of freedom, finally! [I am assuming
we are of the same mind.]) Now I am pedaling a rickety recumbent
bicycle through insomnia, desperately attempting
to wear myself out, listening to Mozart for sonic restitution:
Forgive me, Wolfgang, it's been too long. I will find you
and you will tell me about the room in which you were born.
Though I should warn you, ineptitude, that I know everything
there is to know about canned fruits and veggies, I used to
work in a cannery. That's something you'll have to imagine,
cause I quit and won't go back. I can tell you that
being in the presence of good people, you become better—
I should know, I am one of those sponges. If you cannot admit
your luck, then you're unworthy, someone said, high
on a night of excess, added that sometimes you get it right
when you're trying to get it right.
                                        How many letters have I written
in the shower and never sent? There's nothing much like the cure
of a lathered rant with the label of a Mexican beer
peeling in the soapdish. About those whales, they'll have to wait.
First I must admit the three stages of failure: pride, denial,
indifference. That's dumbing it down, of course, but we are

already approaching level three. Fix yourself already, she said, we'll be
late to church. Somewhere hidden, a small boy and a tie. His mother
tipping sour orange juice from a champagne flute. Sun pitting
trees against themselves. A burgundy gown. Behind and beneath
the trees, some darkness. When the stubby legs of land-bound whales
grew into fins, they came upon new depths. Even now, miles out,
they break the surface for air, exhale a deep purple gurgle, reminiscent
of quadruped ancestry, the way their great-wolf-whale-ancestors would
crouch on a moonlit crag and howl into the night, look down into stars
dancing blithe across the gentle lapping surface of the future.

JIM DAVIS

After Re-watching Eternal Sunshine
of the Spotless Mind

He sat in the old wicker chair of decades past, a guitar leaned
against the small wooden bookshelf. Rumble of potential
rain. An empty canteen of guacamole and a curled sack
of restaurant-style corn chips. A branch dragging across
the window sill whispered, *I'm second only to knuckles on concrete.*
Show me a smile, baby, please. I want to see the world
with you once more—branches settled, stirred again—

                              go wayward.
                    Poetry is a parking meter, permanently
out-of-order, free, and too good to be true. Service in this town
might be kind, but it's undercut with obligation, you know that
as well as I do. He tugs on the waitress' apron strings. *Do your taxes*
have to be filed at the same time each year? she asked, surprised,
looking up from her watercolor of the Carolina sky—*I call it "Barbeque*
Horizon"—*d'you like it?* It was difficult to see the relevance in her
line of question, but every man in the world would have nodded.
                              She hugged him
and he spent the night, found himself pulling on pants one leg at a time
(two attempts at the left), in the hallway, clutching his keys
so they wouldn't ring, rubbing lack of sleep from his eyes.
          When was the last time? Three years? Me too. Maybe more.
Just watched it again—her name escapes him—*you haven't died*
your hair blue, have you? Winter birds. Sleeping birds. Winter provision
held until it broke, admiring the harsh patterns of frost
in the manner of a man who's cut himself to pieces
in the mirror. Huddled, they shake rime from their feathers.
(He tried to forget *meet me in Montauk*

ASSUMPTION

but he was reminded.) Hesitant, penetrating
the world—it's only "mindbending" the first time around.
And even that's a stretch.
Watched it last night and it stuck with me all day, he said.
The weather is the weather.   No reply.
The good cry of what nothing has prepared you for: the pigeon
falling from hibernation, smashed to bits on an unforgiving sidewalk.
The hawk tucked into its wings – nothing has ever been willing to give
itself to this. Pepper. Cold risotto.
                    Forgive the dissolution of a face, the devolution
of expression: unexceptional, unforgettable, unprepared—
dripping like a flag from its pole in the cold. Ex-patriots
in the wilderness we decide to walk into and against.

            He's walking now in tire tracks again, heel to toe, the sour smell
of rot spilling from a dumpster. Another empty alleyway. I'm too old for this,
                                he said, in lines of steam rising
at the fractal edge of misery and blissful nonexistence.

Psychoanalysis of Fire Eaters

He gagged and you ordered Pad Thai Chicken.
I ordered the night on a plate of black beans.
There's no one in this restaurant who can tell me
what any of this means. Now I've gone and done
everything I told you I might. But the truth is
ambitions are mostly lies—there's psychology
to prove or disprove it. I wandered into the woods
with two sticks of dynamite and a magnifying glass,
a copy of Moby Dick. By the fire we compare cherry scars,
yours much sweeter for the wear—mine the bulb of a stoked cigar
ember pressed into flesh—once, then again. Why not press
the button for every elevator floor and hope the best?
Do the things you wanted to do when you were young.
I wanted to write books. I wanted to scatter alternatives.
I wanted to focus on you and us but return to this:
my sister nearly died, and if that's not an excuse
then I'm fine, god of histories, just fine—let's not
play that game twice. On her most recent birthday
we had breakfast: bacon, eggs, apple pancake. What did we
dream about as children? I wonder at the ember and flicker of fire –
we all do, truly, says Bachelard—it can be the pit dug in the wood,
or the teardrop on the wick of candle driven through the sweet glaze
of an apple pancake. Let's not play that game again, I said, until
at least the grays have claimed the tower of our scalps, and all those
older whites have died off, assumed the natural order, descending,
if you please. I said this then to interrupt our conversation, my
staring into the black iron crisscross tables collecting rain, empty—
want for shakers, sugars and cream, a roll of silverware

ASSUMPTION

and a small cut daisy. I'd take a small candle, were you still here,
and melt in your momentary warmth, your trifling radiance,
if I weren't so distracted all the time and did I mention
I miss you terribly and it's only just finished raining?
and my teeth and tongue and throat are charred?

Imagining the Fracture of Modern Disorder

lavender and gunneries
the specific scent of smelting from the iron forge

six hours of sleep isn't nearly enough; eight seems to be
    too much
           the rebooting process exaggerates
              pity
shower curtain liner, white
            is torn
        gives a glimpse into the underside
     of a blue striped curtain
          sparks disease
which we see in dreams as sea urchin
     nesting on healthy cells

is it a lie to write about things you imagine
    you'll die from? what
    will the poets do, if so? inclined
wheelchair ramps—rolled away, a list of fears would be too
           familiar—I am here
to capture the fragmentation of an early afternoon
revisit: the old neighborhood, where I used to write
about the old neighborhood, sitting on a park bench
at an alternate time-stop, a gap in the aforementioned nostalgia—
the bench is peeling, isn't, then is— have we come to know things
              only to reinvent them?
Sunday morning, woke two hours late with two feet
on the floor, shirtless, shoes on and all the apartment lights humming

ASSUMPTION

a dog barked down the way, that was all
the great city morning had to offer, making pigeons out of doves

his uncle played in the minors, Oakland A's farm system, drafted
late in '83, said he couldn't swing his way out of a paper bag, he said
play guitar acoustically, at first, sing in the shower, you'll need something
once you've whittled down worry to a splinter

sound of rumbling luggage
sound of hickory splintering
sound of the overwhelmed
                        and the whelming helpless

when all goes to hell, find the rhythm of a Big-Leaguer
in the cadence of your walk

JIM DAVIS

Wells on Welles, an Orison

We prayed for a miracle...

KTSA San Antonio, reporting.

       The able bodied sons of these United States
dug into their gun collections. Orson Welles' delivery
of our infinite complacence, our general spinning, neglecting
the vast intellectual promise of the occupied universe,
stirred those tuned in.
          Standing on the stoop of an English cottage, smoking a pipe
and staring into the late blue afternoon, which allows
                            preview of the night's moon: pale
pocked face where lakes might once have been,
H.G. wonders at the crawling night worms, half naked
in the mud—hours later, squirming slaves to lunar pull,
dancing and pointing, threatening consciousness.

[We interrupt this broadcast to volunteer
the idea that Jesuit college preparation
offers the children of pilgrims
opportunity to discover, that is, to invent, language:
find communication unique to and of themselves/itself.]

Down on Oak Street, the Johnston's 1930 American Cathedral radio, carved walnut, is
polished and humming. Boys on their bellies and elbows, staring into the countdown, the
inevitable collision with New York. Oh, the desperation: meatloaf perfuming the kitchen,
drifting to the den: what is left for us? Frankie Wilson rode the coattails of Elliot Ness to finally
catch the untouchable thug, the atom's been split, prohibition is over, and someone in Scotland

spotted the Loch Ness monster, unrelated to Elliot's role in the imprisonment of Capone, but interesting,

nonetheless. Plus, the lumps have been pressed from mashed potatoes, something mothers usually forget.

To stir the pot, H.G. and Orson meet for the first time
in 1940, less than one year after the commencement of WWII.
Two years after Welles read Wells to the patient, exited United States.
There are no mistakes
in public speaking, (presuming sincerity, humanity's only charm: blunders
hurdled by Jesuits, prepped for communication
by communication). Requisite error. Rebirth.
Snake with tail in mouth: Ouroboros, if only
movement could be assumed.

[*piano interlude*]

Brigadier General Montgomery Smith
mentions Grover's Mill, is distracted
by the Empire Penguin
painted on the door of the ice delivery truck

which has melted. Conjectural. Our downfall
is the mastery of language. Oration. That is, we have been
too accurate, which is to say
too time consuming to possibly be efficient.
[The devolution of language is progress.]
Wells, our current selves in latent state, waiting

for binary thought to click and pop our tongues.

Henceforth, the furtive existence of a lonely derelict
will carve itself beneath the highway overpass in water stains
that shape the Madonna, wetting bouquets placed at her feet.
                                        Whetting dissonant tongues.

Conversation is all we are
after. Language in piles of rubble
where we might as well construct.

—*If it's amusement you're after, I guess the game's up.*
—*What is there left?*

Efficiency, though I wish there was a better way to say
efficient. Better, faster, stronger.

Fruitless examples. Radio waves. Eternal progress, until,
thank Heaven, here appears, as seen
from the stained oak deck of the author

rising through waves of outrageous heat
one small red squirrel in a beech tree.

ASSUMPTION

City of Springs

When all the light in the city came from a can
they held their hands over, he broke a bottle over his head
and collected the pieces in a velvet purse. Standers
by the way took pictures as he brought forth a sort of cry,
victory over tempered glass. The next morning,
he picked small shards from his scalp, matted with blood.
For years he buried himself in living and reliving.
Telling always master of fortune and deed,
an elevated sense of the semi-accomplished. Sometime
in his late twenties, he found his first gray hair—it sprung
from his palm when the blue-gray wagon pulled out of the drive.
Standing on the asphalt in sudden rain, he felt a flash
of recollection, of backseat indiscretion, impulse revisited.
Never to be visited again. Smoke. In a stone compartment
under the highway overpass, curtains, and the gray came up
like an exponential seed, hulking sprout, strangling the air
and dirt and the very sun that made it. From his bag of broken
glass, he unsheathed a jagged tooth, green to protect its former
contents from light, traced a seam in the couch in the den.
He peels back its floral skin, blue and yellow, faded,
and climbs inside. Dark, coiled towers, he wears the new
beginning like a crown, proud to be beaten, the most
furious of cushion lumps. Years bleed away and the postscript
never arrives. Shut the lights off, if you're brave, squint.
Once everything's gone dark you might see him move again.

Two.

The moon from any window is one part whoever's looking.
                    —Li-Young Lee, *Book of My Nights*

Kissing a rose is a dumb thing to do
not just from the rose's point of view.
But it's a start
like driving off a cliff's probably a finish.
                    —Dean Young, *Primitive Mentor*

On Method

It begins with birds above a maple tree.

Stance: sincere expression of distaste
regarding improper use of language
concealed in commanded hypothetical

sketching its already exaggerated
orifice of the human body
as it relates to the human condition

paralleled in familiar image
turned on its head, shaken
by a drop of blood: a fury.

Reflect upon the odds
and the nature of disorder, worry
and rant about savages, who

have carved their way into history.
Scrubbed, lathered, and rinsed.
Who has not behaved improperly

when manipulating another's tongue?
Who is not a product of fusion, alive
in the smoke ring halos of the undivided?

Then again, the birds.

On Grit

Dray pulling pallets of soy.
Knees of blue jeans worn and gray.
Shirtless, dry hay stalk bowing
from his teeth. The boy looks past
the lip of the mouth of the well
holding a reed-thatched bucket at length
as a lone hawk slices through silver sky
in search of farm rats, mouths slick with yolk
as they scurry from the hen house, thieves.

The boy swats a horsefly
as the truck appears, inspiring
red waves of dust and clay—
confident hand cupped
behind his patient ear.

On Campbell McGrath's Time

Campbell please, take a seat, I've been meaning to do this
for a while now.
I'm here with you, and for you, even if I am against
your time, I am on it.

Mostly because of the fumbling forward, the malfunctioning
headlamp—that's the easy part, we all do that, it's the motion-
lights on the back porch that ring awake, uncertain
what they've found … that's my insomnia—it's memory
that's flawed, it's the balance of reverence and progress
which shimmies through elusion.

Anyone can tell you it's raining. That's cleansing simplicity.
Absolution, however …

As if you stumbled into the dinner party drunk,
soft hat under your arm, your beard a nest, rheumy-eyed,
breathing sour whiskey, forgetting names—until, after
tenderloin, before profiteroles, you stand, holier now,
to sing us a sad song with your eyes closed, and win us back.

That's you, Campbell, more or less
when you admit, pages later,
regarding time, that

It is the house of this moment.
Pertaining, perhaps, to the trees
or the reaches of tree now skirting along the window ledge,

or their eventual souring carcasses.
We live in it now, you say
as another sad song spins absently
and you pluck your umbrella from the stand.

ASSUMPTION

On Distinguishing Flaming Lips From Jane's Addiction

Smoked salmon is stretched over the breadth of a poppy
bagel, sliced and toasted, glowing in its oil like a flat
tangerine, juicy and slick, like the Dickman goldfish,
(Matthew, you're welcome), or what the unwitting love interest
of Wayne Coyne used to dye her hair. I've seen him recently
sharing a NASA flight test with Stephen Colbert—separate
of course, from Perry Ferrell, who's been caught stealing
more times than one—atonement is a fantastic distraction.
What's not stolen, I've decided, has only been mis- or re-
interpreted. Hass used "cordage" in Envy of Other People's Poems—
never mind the insertion of himself, plaited within the core
of Homer's heroic hexameter—he stole the word from Frank
O'Hara, pining to the Harbormaster ... and I will use it to
describe a night spent with a Cuban ex-gymnast, I will feel
like a thief, even swaddled in the unique quilt of my telling,
since I've seen the word twice before, I'll carve it with a spike
into a small chamber in Spain: orange blossoms—the cordage
of scarves and belts—thumping in rhythm and moan of Jane's
Addiction or Flaming Lips—I love this song, she said—sweating
tying her hair back with a band from her wrist—on the ledge
a collection of birds tucked into their wings—the sea braiding
itself into knots through the night. The difference, she thinks
is in the way one moves, or allows herself to be moved, that
the heaviness of envy, tied like an anchor to a man, will sink him
and the harmony he assumes. Yoshimi ties herself to nights past
and drags him along—this and other nights, sinking like a palm-
ful of vitamins and static stretch. Fighting memory with a tire iron
while Wayne breathes fire. You should have seen the terror

of winter lost to Spanish summer and palm trees lit
with fire of industry and a young girl's yin yang face: divided
beside the trembling hands of lonely growing old. Get back at it,
I told myself, shaking the image of salmon spread over the breadth
of a toasted bagel, a book of open poetry, and some familiar song
crackling over the radio, one of two bands we used to admire.

Jug of Milk

An old man sits on the top step,
spitting seeds into the alleyway.
The swing is broken. The trees cannot
offer shelter from rain,
but a sprawling web
of shadow on sidewalk.
The milk jug split in the fall, and spilled
along its thickest flank, thumped and puddling
in the drive. Dark pieces of floating leaf.
Darkness made the dead-bolt stubborn.
The door-mat is peppered with leaf bits.
I snapped a rubber band around the lip
of a container covered in cheesecloth
and filtered myself a glass of milk.
An old man is hassled in the driveway
and a neighbor is stabbed in his heart,
defending. Everything is a metaphor
for everything. A woman among the harbor rocks,
skipping stones. She hides a long lock of hair
behind her ear and wonders
how possibly it could ever
be all so complicated as that.

JIM DAVIS

The Assumption of the Philosopher Upon the Universe

I, man, we are both desired and essential
and must devote our entireties to pursuits
of evidence thereof.

Only after the admission of mistakes
can a mistake be made. Admission: indirect
quality of conditionals, as in, one cannot break
an unidentified condition.

Mostly, in such naming, under such consideration,
we label Language, God, and us, we, I, the gods of language
are elevated—as such, our apotheosis—thus, we are
both desired and essential
in a universe of our own design

painting our savage names on brick, panel, aluminum flanks
of dumpsters rumbling with foraging rats
peeking out with beady eyes to bask in awe of the moon or a glaring
night club marquee, blinking with divinity.

Bicycle wire. Chains.
Sidewalk cracks and hand grenades.
Angled shatterings.
Summer shorts, where less is more.
And cigarettes, when more is less.

Spin the spiderlike web of connectivity.
Paper cups stained pink at the rim. Gasoline

ASSUMPTION

as weapon or spectrum of color in a puddle
when the hydrant cap is missing.
And those rats, glossed over from brandy cakes, frozen
if only for a moment, in a stitch of universal kinship, then

scattered by the clap of a car door, or the swivel of sunset
as the world turns to its back once more. As we begin
to speak supremely of it.

Sleepless, Thinking of Gods

It takes but a night of ill thought, damaged sleep
to dry the fruits of language. The morning has been
prosperous, blessed by the forged hand of Demeter, foretelling
Persephone's return—when wheatgrass stabs through dirt,
springs forth from fields to grow with clover and dandelion
sprouts, begs the leaves to shake awake, cricket spring
and sing to life—but the day has cast its recalcitrant cold
over brick and broad shoulders of the city and its shadow.
Lay me down, she says, and can think of nothing else to say.
It's true we all require a spark, a small handful of fruit—
not the hard, dry pear of seasons past. Then go, she said,
insisting insomnia go 'way from such repast. Feed yourself
on the last ladybug of the season, strawberry beetle, tapping at the lamp.

In the silence of the parkway, Poseidon
split the cap of structure with an axe,
or a hammer and wedge (it is difficult
to examine the victim in shadow).

Just then, surrounding trees discovered one another,
became the plaited lengths of wisdom and compassion,
through the emergence of a method like human circulation,
like the branching of consciousness through gray matter.

Spider; spider, crawling through histories, it only takes one
night of damaged sleep to suck imagination dry.
Sisyphus found himself surrounded by everyman, how all
must lonely be—not so stuck in a web hanging lithe from a tree,
but sitting on a stubborn stone, stroking Cerberus between the ears
and sipping at the cool juice of language he's learned to squeeze.

An Episode of War

It's important to leave the orchard
in the early morning, before the bugs arrive, said Ares,
stretching and yawning after a nap. I invented, he said,
Arachnophobia, among other things—there was a girl
in Mrs. Needleman's fourth period bio class who stuck
gum on the underside of his desk. Her name was Arachnid,
oddly enough, those were the days when new parents took pride
in a name's ingenuity—the final moment of complete control.
Her parents owned a cherry orchard, but they were sour
and bruised after any big wind. They shared a Coke
one afternoon on the bank of the Euphrates, it was too warm
for coffee. Have you noticed the purple trees they've planted
at the Acropolis? How the sky is redder than it's ever been?
(A boar snorted about the forest for truffles, ate many things.)
It's morning again, and she's left him for a software salesman
outside of Monterrey. He took up golf and archery, abandoned croquet
but found himself in songwriting, plucking the golden mandolin he stole
from his father, who has always been unfairly particular
about sending his other-worldly possessions on loan. Anyway, one day
his neighbor, Dan—six foot eight—a man whose knees ached
from the weight and angle of his limbs, slightly knotted
from a disease which Ares referred to as "the gangle"
plucked him from the snow by the collar. Ares unbolted a bloodshot eye
and fell into a rant about advertising in baseball, these days, how
if a man can get on base and stay there, he's worth every penny. A whisper
that screamed of sour whiskey. He said one day, when he was eight or nine,
a wolf spider crawled from the outhouse bench and bit him behind
the knee. He's been working on his short game, he said, but it was slurred,
so Dan lowered him back into the snow, knowing full well
that once everything had melted and the sun took proper arc, that Ares
would return to the orchard, to nap in the shade of a tree, or perch in a limb
with the half-eaten body of a lamb hanging limp between his teeth.

Liminal

The threshold
of a poet's work—
the moment
when a blade of grass
becomes a king—
a drop of dew
his crown—
the moment
somehow neither
and both.

Lamentation of Anteros

I could study in the shadows for a lifetime
so I'd never need confront the light.
Caught in the downdraft, under the eave, I wonder
what was given me by masters of sweetbreads,
of pig-face rolled in cheesecloth and boiled?
Gimme a taste of that, she said, do not end your sentences
with propositions, or begin a line with conjunction
or stir a siren sleeping, you have no idea
how tired one must be to use a concrete step
as a pillow. Pressed against the face of an old man,
another face—his daughter by his bedside, the only one
to tell him of the pigeon on the sill and the flock of geese
landing on the lawn, braking their downturned tails
hard against the breath of another long winter
rising from the grass—they've come back, she said.
There is wonder in the telling of how it ought to be, and grief.
(Born to hunt like brother Eros, what was given
by my maker in a quiver of leaden arrows?)
First the honking, then the snore of a man inching into shadow. Why—
good gods all mighty—why do I always paint my way
into a deathbed? What poetry is that? I wonder
to a notebook after my third cup of decaf and cream
at the Clarke's on North Damen, on the night of nothing much at all,
like most nights, which is why I order apple pecan pancakes
for a change, and do my best to forget it's raining. Who is
raining? And wouldn't some poetry be nice?
Another peeled creamer lid. One more stirring spoon.
We'll have to wait for this rain, or the sound of rain to stop—

as if there were anyone to notice the difference, one whose
armor's pierced and bleeding, or not, or someone in between.
A man and woman running through traffic with newspapers
held above their heads, holding hands. Shriek of thunder.
Talk to me, good gods, she said, this will only take a moment.

Sunday Morning Coming Down

Wasn't there some mention of getting brunch?
That's the Chicago thing to say: let's get brunch.
It means eat and drink away a hangover. 57 degrees
on the morning we wore shorts without showering, after coffee
and sun shades. It'll pass. Every current sandwich is named
for an artist. I order the Klimt without Ranch, surprised by red onion.
Barely 3 o'clock, the sun already threatens departure. When you spoke
this morning you conjured a campfire, embers spilling like coins
from the shadow in a mouth of a flickering shadow. Aspirin. Two cans
of Big Flats. Haircut? We'll see. Wandering the Walgreens on Milwaukee.
I pass on hand warmers, read local scores in the pages of another dying paper.
Note the phrase *fall in wonder at*. A woman near the magazine rack
has just finished crying. It's not like me to admit the Macadamia Oil
Conditioner I buy, but anyone who has come this far deserves to know.
I make a list of projects in the margin. I hope to write a poem.
I read and gather the proceeds of methods preceding. I ration my paychecks
meagerly. I am ambitious in my spending and I can't quite remember
the first half of the day and did we ever go to eat? I'm starving and only
as drunk as a solo drunk allows, simmering at the level of forgetfulness.
The songs I wrote one summer on postcards home from camp, scribbled
on the flayed backs of white-skin trees. Song titles: Wisconsin Tissue
was one. I remember still the words and rhythm and I didn't go number two
for a week and if you slept through breakfast you got thrown in the lake.
We played capture the flag and won and I grabbed the last flag and held it up
and hollered like a scalp-taker and felt good but never wanted to go back.
And did someone mention brunch? It's darker than it was and growing cold.
Wolfgang Amadeus, who are you? And have you seen the pancakes
at the Golden Apple? They're not the same as S&Gs, where cherries dot the eyes
and buttermilk flapjacks flash pineapple smiles. All day it's true my mind has not
been right.   Wolfgang, can you hear me? Why do you
ring here in the diner, where a beautiful girl hangs photographs of ivy flowers

and cattails bowing at a green river—would you ring the same in the ears
of brown bears hibernating? Nimble through caves, great pockets of stink and snore?
That's a stupid thing to say, Wolfgang, I'm sorry. It's just that I am
hungry and nostalgic and still a bit hungover and if I were to start with the details
I might not ever get the details straight. And I am having trouble seeing
the difference between liberty and lonely, mostly in the way they are written,
sung, and played. The red beans here are fine. They go well with memories
carved in birch bark and buried.

Fennel

In the script of the window screen, covering the heavy bulk
of the brick wall beyond, groping through the dark of near-wake,
I write wonderful nothings, funnel craft into blame: who was
this Pheidippides, the man who ran to Athens to tattle
on the Persians, to someday save the Greeks? Rejoice! Rejoice!

No one mentioned Pheidippides was blind drunk. Whiskey
as alchemy, he said, it turns the world gold, rubbing some on
his bottom lip. Trust me on this. You are born of the ocean,
she said, tracing her tongue along the ridge of his cheekbone.

Wherefrom she arrived alludes him, whichever origin we
decide, will not be bothered by concision, will hold tight to
the impressions of light off the wave-backs as wind gathers tide,
disturbed like the inclination of wind chimes. Pheidippides
agrees with the riverbeds left in her eternal skin. Un-

touchable, she, whose father burned the horses with the stable.
Remember when snow was clean and appealing? Remember that
December she spent days in the den with her head between her knees?
And by the time he returned from sleepwalking she'd extinguished

the sky of their making, she, on the business end of a stick
whittled to a point—her sweet flames, her char, the smoke rings rising.
Still I write her into songs. I wish there was something short of
marathon effort, like tracing blooms in a field of fennel
painted gold, some system to replace my face against the bars.

Temperance

He dipped his brush in crimson oil to paint an empty pail.
How can you tell from this angle? Turn on the light, she said.
A bucket? Yes. *And is that a dog?* Yes. It's a dog.
There's flaw in your stroke, it's convincing, it makes me want
to tube a newspaper, strike her haunch. Careful, he said,
headlines are decidedly harder these days. They laughed,
he fingered the canal between her knuckle and wrist,
she smiled, turned back to the canvas and touched it.
Strokes dried to points like colored teeth. I've got one, he said.
What's the difference between wind through a pail,
and thread through the eye of a button?
She sipped a plastic cup of wine, trying to decipher chardonnay
from pinot, shrugged (if it's not from a box, it's probably fine).
A vehicle, she said, *a co-operative attachment, while the other is free*
to focus its attention on lack of contents. His mind was fuzzy
from linseed oil and sauvignon. She smiled, grabbed him
by the collar, pushed him back into the couch and knelt.

Years later, they have fallen out of touch.
She calls him on a Sunday as it rains.
How could you paint an empty pail? It's not possible
to paint emptiness, to capture absence. You'd have to be mad
to spend your life on such things. Baby, he whispers—
he can tell she is crying, he imagines the cord
wrapped around her finger, and she, in a distant city
would be wearing a summer dress, Roman sandals
laced up her calf, sunglasses pinned in her hair—
I won't upset you, neither would I hope to paint what's not there.
I'm trying to call attention to the hole in the bucket.
You don't need to see the puddle to understand.

ASSUMPTION

A dog scratches at the door. He stretches to turn the handle,
clutching the receiver between his shoulder and chin.
Is that Maggie? Yes. *How is she?* Fine, just fine.
He'd given up drinking the year before, set a ringed mug
of coffee on the countertop. The dog attacked its water dish.

I guess I never thought of it that way, to paint what's missing.
Believe me, he said, I understand, but that's how it has to be—
what else can we hope for, if not what is, or isn't?

The dog sat watching him fiddle with the cord, smiled,
tilted its head, then shook its dripping jowls on the floor.

Briar

The woman with one hundred hands
swatting wasps through an afternoon
is immune to their barbed insistence
and to whiskey barreled and shook
from the belly of the horse drawn cart
that took at the knee the leg of the Johnson boy
one dark cold morning as he collected
coal from cobblestone creases
a penny for a lump the size of a fist.

Come evening, when he arrived
smelling of cigars and sour mash
ambling down the hall with a wooden gait—
she waited for his sonorous dreams
to straddle his chest and press
one hundred loaded pistols to the ribs above his heart.

Years later, slow and fire-hardened
sitting round the hearth with the boys
tin cans ember red and gray upon the logs
comparing scars and stories of scars
when he pulled up his shirt, displaying craters
white and raised—please, he said, smiling ...
remember this one? Just then, something
stirred in the briar, and even the moon was lost
in her embrace, dodging thorns and thatched branches

of the nest he has tried to but never escaped.
In the bones of her liking, the dry grasp of providence.

ASSUMPTION

Panhandle

Selene solicits a couple lunching on the patio at Luigi's
Italian Eatery. They were a sharing a sandwich
of shaved turkey, peppercorn cheese melted into focaccia
with pesto mayonnaise. I don't have anything, she assured him,
I've spent too long in the woods. My granddaddy always told me
you gotta learn how to fight before I'll teach you
to talk like a scoundrel, young lady. Sorry, I didn't mean to
bring the crazies around (ain't no furies like the first),
it's these new eyes I'm seein' with—my first time in a big city.
The couple shifted in their seats, glanced at each other, Selene.
No way, she exclaimed, noting the stack of books on the elbow
of the tabletop, I write too! I write songs, plays, novels, I write
movie books ... the key is to write only what you know, show 'em
what you got, see if it sticks—like spaghetti, my gramma used to say.
She had a face tattoo that was just beginning to scab, a scarab
and a palm leaf. You a poet? she said. How's this, you don't want to know
what I done. I done just about everything—how poetic is that?
Brother, she said to the man, clearly taken aback, I been in prison
for ten years before this, outside three weeks now, and I ain't goin back.
Take my cratered lakes, take my Mare Isularum and swim in it.
I gotta find a way downtown, she said, you got some change? you know
when the bus run? Good luck, said the couple. You know where "luck" come
from ... Lucifer! I'm gonna bless myself instead, brother, hiking up
the strap of her shoulder bag, closer to her neck, where another tattoo was
peeking up from her collar, also scabbed. Now all I need is two
frickin dollars for a guitar string, she slurred, finishing a can of beer
with a belch. Ah now, don't even bother, I'll go find myself a shade tree
and rest for a while. Later that night, thousands stand on balconies
across the city, catching the echoes of a song played from a park bench,
splitting the limbs of a shade tree with divine pallor, lunacy, a chorus
aching its way across the key of B, negotiating the entire minor scale,
until, finally, vibrating lights brought the evening to her knees.

Caveat

the third man
in the chorus sings
let him beware

falling higher
than the dyadic
river's auspice

my transparency, river rocks
your reflection, distant suns

eyes closed, entreating
the audience hushed
among the reads

I told you this would hurt
you said, as if you were dreaming

Say Again

They cut across the city saying nothing, mismatching strides.
He much taller than she. It's a dream he has woken from
many times before, it seems, though whenever he enters
the red stone deli in Uffhausen, he is struck by the contents
of a glass display case—everything cured, cylindrical,
pastel and earth toned: long tubes of meat: smoked ham,
braised roast-loaf, veggie-loaf with small bits of color floating
in clear gelatin, not the artificial clot, the real scum scraped
from boiled hooves and teeth. They left with lunch wrapped
in crisp paper and ate while studying a map, the clock tower
shadows stretched over the city, strangle aching tenements and up
the hill where armies once traded blows. It was a nice place
to sit and drink, to see the lustrous river snaking through.
He said, there is no place in the world I would rather be
than right here, right now, with you. She bristled and he resigned
to rid himself of clichés. German crows perched in a tilted beech.
An old woman once told him, while weeping at the banks
of the Seine, painting water lily portraits for crust and wine,
that clichés were no different than any adjective—the German
Warmblood is strong and fast, the river is silver and singing—*say again*
What were you thinking? *say again* Were I to kneel and grovel
would you admit that what is novel and accurate will be repeated,
will come to be known as truth, will be repeated, repeated, overused,
disdained, unused over tongues of the creative, only to reappear,
fashionable, retroactive truths applied to a different time.
                                        Two different stride lengths,
swinging hands like a flawed metronome, setting the old song
to syncopation, to reinvention. As far as he recalls, the hill
was distinctly purple that day, for some reason, and the vistas

pocked with wondrous green, thunderous clock towers reaching
through them to a chorus of spindles and gears of hyperbole.
He truly believed, sitting on the lip of a stone barricade
in such company, that he was exactly where he was meant to be.
When the crows lifted, the beech tree shivered in perpetuity,
the hands of the clock tower froze, and the town wept when it woke.

ASSUMPTION

Luigi's Famous Submarine Sandwich:

ham, salami, capocollo, provolone,
lettuce, tomato, basil and oil. Giovanni Martinelli
building through the speakers of the deli.

He's always around, the owner, parked in the corner
of the tight corner bistro, or parked in the no-parking zone
unloading branches of fresh bread, sacks of peppers and onions.

The only universal being the onerous connection, layered
webbing, skeins of thought—as I sink my teeth into the crust
of stacked, salted meats and cheese, in my mind I return
to a pool party on the northern border of Michiana, the Italian
sub that burned the lip and throat sores I'd developed
that summer away at camp. Arms and ankles pocked with spider-
bites that would be egg-sacks, my cousin teased, but were not
and I was not immune to sun, pink, and certain strains
of oral disease. I found out recently the affluent family
in whose pool we were asked to party, fell apart, literally.
She toppled over a hotel balcony after a fight. And he, escaping
grief, he explained, skiing the Swiss alps, went headfirst into a tree—
woozy on schnapps and amphetamines, dressed like an 80s movie,
bright and striped and patterned. Now dead. And the young son
offed himself in the basement with a belt strapped to a pipe.
That's what they were fighting over that night, they said
when she went headfirst into the hotel pool—didn't they already
have one at home? I didn't understand. There is nothing
to link Luigi's Famous Italian sandwich to suicide. You'll have to
pry this cannoli from my cold dead hand, said a female voice
at the next table over. The owner, Biagino, tapped his loafer-toe

to the undercurrent of Martinelli's opera drifting toward coda.
His father, on the farm in Bari, came in from a summer storm
and said You have to pack your things, 'Gino, this life is not yours.
And it wasn't. And it is. And he asks himself, nightly,
over cannoli and decaf, if he would forfeit depth of thought
for a wealth of experience? trade it all for a small brown ratsnake
weaving through the vineyards, nesting in the loft above the barn?

Dolls

Broken photos buried in the cellar
of the dollhouse, under unsent letters.
The tiny, broken home—you should see it
when the cord of the naked bulb is pulled
and it clicks, and it hisses with ominous filament,
and it shakes. Tiny broken figurines. Please believe
that this is not the story of one wounded, more
the song of one who's spent a lifetime
discovering a cure for the common
dogbite, or would like to—punctures of any sort would do:
cavernous, hollow, steeping with deep-rooted bacterium
burying amoebic heads into flesh like small tumors
on the haunch of deer traipsing at Aspen altitude
through gritty, unprotected thickets, like an endless
love scratch. What begs mention is the fact
that PhDs sometimes look down upon the page
curious at their own spelling (thier? their? ... *i* before *e* ...)
It only lasts a moment, like the drunk you are
too afraid to spy on through the window, singing in the street.
As for the dollhouse, open the face at the hinge, to see
inside, to free the rooms of must, though I have to warn you
that fear will be the same, a slightly different pitch in the song
fading out like the tooth-sunk colophon of puncture wounds.
Gorgons, they say, were modeled after bloated dead.
Deep sunk eyes, dark, swollen, slightly discolored and still.
Loosen the prisoner's tongue, allow him to bend and stretch,
to see the world through stark, unblinking fields of acuity.
At the mouth of anything vicious there is, at least, passion.
There is, at least, a moment, a map dot
where what comes out should be bottled and kept
or posed in broken acceptance at the foot of the bed.

After Slow Dancing With a Girl Who Had a Boyfriend at the Wedding of a Former Colleague

Hungover on the year's most beautiful day, he'll forgo
the ham sandwich for sliced lamb and beef, six piece
falafel, six piece grape leaves. How can you give away a day
        like this, she asked as he napped on the couch in the sun.

Please, said his dream voice, she's not even semi-glossed.
What's with reverie anyway, when he who's been abandoned
is exactor of terrible normalities, feet fraught with concrete—
sorry to burden the process with response. He thinks that
a heavy conscience is less in the haughtily conscious, and he is
        not willing to pay anything over the asking price. If you were to

speak without boundary entirely, follow yourself headfirst
into all and sundry crotch, tipped heavy by sex or the promise of sex …
sure, he's tried it, which is why he understands all the unpublishable
        private literature he's heard of. An afternoon stuck in traffic—this is

the year's most beautiful day—listening to lectures set to brakes,
wailing ambulance announcements and the cry of neighboring radios.
There's an accident at Foster that's slowing the flow of both lanes.
Nothing is pure, he says, more for her than to, but the unquestioned genius
of one who questions genius. Yes, she said, finally, as she ran, one hand
        on her ear, pressed to phone, the other going white at the knuckle

on the strap of her saddling purse, skirt billowing behind her like a flag,
like the tail of information that floats behind the wise, as she races
to capture a train. Let's never do that again, she said, her headache
        battling his. Competition, ambition—those are the oldest and most

ASSUMPTION

deeply rooted parts of the brain, you know. She said that perhaps
nostalgia heightens ambition. She says, *Shit Haystack, you wanna
live forever?* Live in the moment, she says, think outside of it.
He nods at the other end. She stops to see two brown cats
square off, then again at the parkway where a curl of fern is born
       into itself, and the world it will want to forget. (Don't be so dramatic

she tells an echo [he's hung up].) His lone black suit was beaten
to wrinkle in his bag. Toothpaste split. This is it, she says, so damned
beautiful after all. Most went on chasing, though
she walked back to where it all began, sniffed the air,
       buried her head and her hands in the simple dirt of morning.

Essay on a Dream

Sixty one degrees in January, a record,
hoping my khakis will dry in time for work.
The girl I'm seeing says the earth must be
saying something—the earth must have something to say
and this is her fickle tongue. She's younger than I am, hopeless-
ly beautiful. I've burned through the morning's promise
of a nap. Driving to work, thinking of the dream
I woke to, or from—something buzzing with blue
electric fields—the cat creating static where there was no cat.
Dull the lightening, curtain-less window, a small boy
grabs a doorknob, brass, with a catcher's mitt, Rawlings,
viewed through the dreamscape-omnipotence of multiple points—
back-lit, dramatic in the way a dream's only drama exists
in first person, for a day or so, then dies ... in this way the door bursts
open to release an electric blue version of myself, spinning
in his most violent, unseen temperament—something like a song:
Roses, Roses, Roses in piercing electronics, detached voices—an explosion
of terror and static and sensation that cannot be translated to verse, lyric
essay, or conversation, especially that
of two former lovers in the backseat of a taxi ... I say you fit the role
of every character. Or I do. We are
trying our best to pay attention. We are trying to maintain universality,
shy away from the specific.
I am digging myself out from behind the shadow of the blue mountain
that hovers like a cloud over ineffable intersections of electricity
and dream and lack of attention and lightning flashes
and the cat I don't have creating static.
Describe for me the limits of sleep.

ASSUMPTION

Describe the sensation of disposition without mentioning evolution, or divine.
When the foul mood brightens we'll all be fine, she said. Trust me.
Bourbon, bourbon and strong coffee. Outside in the snowy garden, a briar,
a bramble of fathoms, memories melting, and the blue-gray veil of *roses, roses*—
playing over the watched-pot of khakis rattling in the dryer.
In the shadows of the den, the man in his underpants shivers.

Apehouse

The drawing of a horn on a cave wall:
trumpet, spell of blurts, a conversation
at the watering hole, in the company of another: too long
describing his companion: You know Tom, remember
the Cardinals game last summer? When Terry fell in the pool?

Lights click, pop, and halo themselves
as the final day of the year checks its pockets,
grabs keys from the hall table, scans the room
and, satisfied, chokes the last light from itself
by shutting the door. In the dark, the sound of a bolt
snapping into place. Small eyes battling gloom
and boulevards, awnings, choice thoroughfares
flickering blue with crime. Anticipating the existence
of beleaguered happenstance. Figures vaguely shifting
behind the pulled curtains of a day's sentience.

Aware of what's been said beyond conversation,
you may forget the elephant or gorilla
on your back in the room
where a hooting collection of spider monkeys
swings from fixtures—at once hysterical
and depraved; serene, these unnameables
from the half-drunk recollection of night prior.

We'll make maps of where we've been. Music
tells the story as well as any.

ASSUMPTION

Pale ale; champagne. The priory of fools.
Take and satiate me.

The walls now are painted
with dreamscapes.

The Implication of a Pebble

Ripple the skin of a thick lake. Orbit is nothing
compared to the effort and effect of a boulder
rolled down a hill. There is little said of perspective
in the footprint of a beaten town. Now there is a woman
of the night on every dim corner. There are knives
hidden in sock drawers and in the parks,
more experience than imagination.

A woman in an overcoat with nothing underneath
pointed a gun at the man, demanded, in tobacco-slick tongues,
to hand over the starlight and lay face down in the rain.
From her throat she ripped the necklace chain,
pebbles popped and raced across the floor. *Have you heard of
the Rhinoceros Beetle lifting 850 times its own weight*, she said,
own your handicap, as she buried lead in each of his knees.

On the list of greatest fears, we have neglected
the intrepid ivy climbing stucco, the braided steel wires
hammocking above the yard. There are houses on stilts
so we agree that floodwaters are frightening, but no-
body appreciates the spider in the jar, breathing
through holes they punched in drywall.

This is his desk and books. On the table, his wallet and keys.
He wipes away a streak of dust and wonders
why he can no longer see stars in the night sky.
When the marble rolled and shattered the town, a coarse smoke
rose above them, now settling on the desk and books,
the table, the keys, the thin legs of climbing ivy, and of course
the considerable blanket of soil before the stars,
each muted orbit reflected in the thick lake's rippling skin.

North Avenue Abraham

Honest reflection is all he needs
to fix his hair. He says you can pay
a buck for a banana at the coffee shop
or three for a bushel, and throw out the bulk.
He, bathing in the fountain near the overpass,
thinks he'll make millions on a custard alternative
he invented in a dream. In high school he smuggled
contraband, said contra-banned suggests something
is promoted, right? High on lines of crushed pill,
laughing at security. He says you can pray. He's unsure
if he was dealing sex or drugs, maybe both.
He's got a boxer's nose, pug and crooked,
never boxed. He says he's a gold glove
with only a vague idea of its implication: tough
as nails when it comes to intimidation, though
he doesn't like to fight. One man whispers
to a young girl, shakes her hand. If you see crime
don't jump in, he says, if bad guys bother you, call.
If not, we gonna have to sit down and have a long talk.
She brought him a paper cup of tea. Oh God, have mercy,
we don't want sympathy, he said, neglecting the fact that he was
in the business of sympathy. I got a grocery cart, and he up here
tryin to rob me? Riffling through pockets, he's frustrated at his lack
of organization. Motivation ain't a factor. He carried a spring knife
for protection: you can't have it lest you willin' to cut somebody.
In this world I'd rather need it and have it
than need it and not have it … that's wisdom, girl, remember that.
In the deluded convexity of the milk pitcher,
he caught his reflection, pressed the release
on a silver switchcomb, fixed himself right.
Oh yes, he said, oh yes—it's gonna be a helluva night.

JIM DAVIS

To Better Understand the Birds in the Park

This is my love letter to the birds
that hang like ash over fire. Last night
I could not sleep so I buried myself
in blankets, scarf round my neck, still cold,
so I bundled my bedding and slept on the couch.
On the way down the steps I saw one through the window,
sleeping on a park bench. In the shower I heard the upstairs
neighbors having sex. I heard through the wall
someone came in and stole them. Stole what? I thought, the object
obscured by plush dialogue. She's 30, looks pregnant.
The smart one, they used to call her. I see her now and then
when she's walking her dog.

Sure, I'll have a glass before we leave, she said,
and tipped a watering can to the planted fern.
Layers of prophetic, complicated references
continue to surprise the audience, although
now and then, are lost. Please, I can barely carry enough
to survive the winter. Lick the thread
for texture, that's right, test the wool with your tongue.
See if it is fine enough to weave a blanket from, and remember
there are no old souls, only those who have grown
old before their time.

City snow plows rumble in the lot. There's a girl out there,
somewhere, that one of them will marry.
The rest, who knows? If it rains, it rains, they say.
There might never be snow. And in case you were wondering,

ASSUMPTION

there is still a fist of mistletoe hanging from the eave,
though its leaves are brown and wilted.
It works just the same, however,
when you point to it.
With complete understanding of the flooded yard,
I decide that today is the day I will paint my masterpiece.
I will paste one thousand letters to a board
and stand back to critique. I will consider
the metal-drum bonfires in city parks
as a blinking reflection of stars in the sky.
I will connect the assembly bathed in orange light
to the weightless birds hovering above the heat,
assuming once their bellies swell,
they will settle and nest in the trees.

River

I leaned over and held up the page I had been reading.
Excuse me, miss, can you help? What's this word mean: transmute?
She guessed wrong. Still I asked her to dinner, she said she would
meet me in the hotel lobby at the fountain—I know a place, she said.
It was early and I had some writing to do, a short biography
on Toribio Losoya—the Hispanic Texan who stood the Alamo
with pistol and powder-horn, a lesser-known figure
in the shadow of Travis, Crockett, and Bowie.
I did some laundry. I lay my head down and lifted it
an hour later. The sun had set and I resigned
to no longer write about drinking beer, so I ate an apple
and drank two tall beers and went down to the pool
for a swim. The apple kept surprising me with spots,
a sort of interior rot that could not keep me from drawing
parallels to myself. The rest of the cans were in the sink
with a few handfuls of ice, covered in a cold towel.
I swam a few lengths, held the edge and went under.
A quick flash of memory, a weekend in college when I read
my then-girlfriend a line of verse I labored over
so it might sound confident, casual, sincere. She said that's nice
and moved on. I came up for breath and went for a shower.
That evening we met in the lobby at the fountain
near a large framed reproduction of one of Cezanne's Bathers.
I pointed and nodded, she said her young niece
could have painted that, I don't understand
how people survive in that line of work. They don't I said.
At dinner she ordered a plate of ravioli and wine sauce.
I had brisket and potatoes, a small salad and a beer.
I excused myself to the bathroom and left out a side door,

ASSUMPTION

walked along the river for a while, which was nearby, and saw
a number of famous people do ostentatious things.
I saw a single bluebird and sketched a picture of it on the back of a napkin.
I continued walking until, days later, I happened again upon the restaurant.
She was still sitting there, crying. I sat down beside her.
What's the matter? I thought you left, she said.
She knotted napkin, dabbed her nose and smiled. I sat for a while
and ordered a drink and told her about the bluebird. So what do you do?
she asked. I'm a painter, I said. She packed and left before my beer arrived,
moved to Houston, I think, she always wanted to go there. I saw a man
in a white Stetson cowboy hat tap table salt into his beer, so I did the same.
Then I heard the river speak. Yes, I said. Oh yes. Cezanne slid past
in a red canoe. No, green. There, I said, he's done it.
I dipped a brush into the river, and sure enough, it was green.
Green alright, and never-ending.

Shop Owner Pays Local Drunk 5 Bucks to Wash the Windows

Trees have begun their usual winter reach,
naked and hopeful against blue sky. A couple sharing
margherita pizza and a pitcher of cold beer. She makes
a joke, he sips from a mug near empty. Eyes avoiding.
You'll have to listen hard to hear the voice.
Pabst white and blue label peeled by a thumbnail
in jagged ribbons, measuring levels of what it means
to be alone. Slow thump of the Black Keys on the radio.
Ambulance flashes past window expanse and dishes clatter
as they're cleared. None of this seems to be sticking
the way it usually does, the way it once did. Too early
to be suspicious. There are nights when nothing sticks
to either of them, nights of boundless energy and fall,
words fingered in windshield snow. Copper stamped
ornaments of sliding kitchen doors have elevated themselves
with meaning. In San Antonio they told me Lone Star was
the Pabst of the South, so I drank four tallboys alone
in my hotel room, threw a lamp from the balcony and fell
asleep atop the bedsheets, whose threads I couldn't hope
to count. Someone said to see the world
in a single drop of sweat rolling over the shoulder of a bottle,
that's the only reason I bring it up. The girl of my dreams
is standing at the bus stop with her headphones on or in,
which means I must be sleeping. She told me to grind the cherry
tree to bits. The stump is tipped like a petrified squid
escaping from the bin beside the garden, you can see it
from the kitchen where an old man sits, drinks and sings

as if he forgot he was a bird. As if they lost themselves
in the gullies, the soap and suds and brilliant rivulets
of wiping away, and what's wiped, and the handheld squeegee.
Two cabs. A bucketful of beers. And beads of sweat for all.
The voice is lost – who's that talking? said the owl, standing
proud upon the roofline, plaster mold and painted. *Who? Who?*

The Blinding of Samson

Tell me this: tell me something
of street lights, of road construction, of the fine dust
that rises from its work. Press your breast against me
as you even my sideburns. Beyond that, deliver me
from the anecdotal. Allow me to antiquate a phrase:
give it a body, give it discernible cells
of the same holy substance, sprung from the same muck
as Spanish Palms, Pin Oaks, White Moths and Mountain Goats
ramming their curled teeth in heavy cracks; the same cells
of winter drifts, of the muck from which it rose. The rose,
same as the blade plunged into the eye
of the storm. Blinded silence. Tumbleweed,
once the storm has settled. Now, allow me
the cavalier usage of caveat in general
conversation, with coffee, over eggs
and crisp potatoes, tell me to consider the difference,
admire the many moods of the same sound.
Bells chime in the distance. Finally,
regard, as we shake hands, bow to ovation,
the cicada who bloomed late, two seasons past
the swarm, whose ghostly sleeve clings to the windowsill
so close to where it belongs, reminding us
of concentrated opportunity, of its passing.

Presentation

Tucking a stray tress behind her ear, we listen
to every word she says, apart from precision:
7% of government spending goes to education,
compared to 65% on defense. An atrocity, she says.
A black rubber band is coiled like a snake in the grass
of her chestnut hair. Her pants, just tight enough
to recall the Battle of Mons, where the British picked
a fight with German occupants in 1914—I remember this
because, believe it or not, the Canadians liberated the city—
the Canucks saved the day! There's a plaque in the belfry
to prove it. Anyway, she says, moving on
to popular culture: when the safari loses luster, owners turn
to name-brand fashion—that's how it is, how it's always been.
Again, I return to Mons, imagine a river carving a valley
through hill country, where a young boy shepherds
along the rocky crag of pass, sleeps in a ruined Church,
searches for grass so that his herd might eat. Naked
stumps of Douglas fir, severed at the knee.
The window is open, a breeze comes in
from the river. She has neglected, says the shepherd,
that books are less expensive than bombs. By his calculations,
a weapon capable of any respectable damage
must be one hundred thousand times more expensive
than the average book, which would indicate a ratio
of approximately ten thousand seven hundred books/bomb—
dollars which, judging by the amount we spend on defense,
have made us none the wiser. Which is a shame, he decides,
because, tucking the same chestnut tress and gliding to her seat,
she smiles at him, skewing the numbers for good.

Recruiting Adlai

The way a tin can once told its secret
to the tight, unspindled whispers of summer.
The deep purple wine and teeth too tired for talking.
The deprivation and rage we drift slowly into, or under.
Look closer. There is something off about the drop
of handle, relative to mug. The empty, ochre mug
in the painting, speaking to him with its gaping mouth,
singing to the window, married to the crisp air beyond.
They kiss, and then go walking down drowsy streets, a small dogwood
blooms beneath the elevated tracks, shakes purple in the dark, in the cold.
He is far too old to go skipping like this. To go hissing
like rain as it wets pages, spreads small clouds of ink.

                                                    Can you call this a crisis?
He turned like a kingfisher diving, awake and dreaming of coming to
midway through the operation. Hibernation, ghosts,
the shadow of a window fan on the wall.

He hears hooves beating the earth, somewhere in the distance,
with bass enough to shake us all, if we were paying attention.
Don't wait for translation! he panted. Answer "yes" or "no"!
The city groans and begs for spring. The heat refuses to heat,
the sink leaks, and there's black mold blooming through drywall,
crawling along the floorboards. The free papers roll like tumbleweed, threaten rain.
The L train shakes everything.
The dog in the apartment below is barking
to the dog in the apartment above.
And when the alarm chimes the sun shines demurely in the window.
He will wait as long as it takes.

ASSUMPTION

And I'll stay here, Adlai.
Growing old, growing old and hoping
that the good Lord, sitting beneath the lamp post in the cold,
is patient enough for me
to find my way through the trees, weave
through the orchard and stumble upon the clearing
where warhorses snort and clomp.
Where clouds of smoke are spurred by their stirring.
I will feed them apples, chew a stalk of hay,
stroke their long faces
to calm them.

Old Weather

When I look over my shoulder
into the speckled mirror, I can see the past
two years, covered in a blanket of fresh snow,
else a snow is on the way. I don't smell lilies
the way I used to, which I assume is due
to all the frost. Remember the backpack epidemic?
they'll say, when they speak of us, laughing
at the hunchbacked computer programmer
navigating the hallways as if pressing against
arctic windsheer, clutching the impulse of a mug
programmed to tickle the heat sensitive nerve endings
in a booth full of delicate hands. When it comes to black
& white squares, fresh from the confectioner's oven,
we said, what's the harm in another? I will find
the infrastructure I am after. I wish I was better
at believing. I wish I could forget selectively, instead
of all at once. And since the major damage has been done,
what else is there to do but forfeit to the logic
that sometimes a generous relieving is better
than accurate reliving. The rain has come, is coming
and sooner or later it will wear the hill to a nub like a poet
grinding down his teeth, to expose the catacombs beneath,
lined with veins of nitre and gold, where the buried
only hope to lie long enough to be forgotten. I know
there's no great happiness in forgetting, even when
the pain is less, even when the rain collects familiar dregs
to reawaken—and pollen, and hail, and ash—poised
at the top of the hill, now coming down in sheets.

Elbows and Belly

        pressed into the floor, past my bedtime, two fists
propping my chin, watching X-Files, too young to understand
the subtle exchange of glance between Agents Mulder and Scully—
not until Gillian Anderson appeared on the cover of a men's magazine
        some years later, would I. Young, you'll dive into anything
potentially sweet, so if you see a candy wrapper that looks attacked
by some wild thing, expect to find the culprit nearby, milky
chocolate streaks announcing crime scene and mastermind.
        If you can't find him immediately, check under the bed.

Lesson learned: you find what you're looking for
through investigation, categorization, and imposition, it won't hold
up in court, but it'll have to do. As George Oppen said, likely
        in reference to an incomprehensible interconnectedness,
things explain each other, not themselves.

By eight o'clock the sky is ripe for picture taking.
Buildings have ruddied their cheeks with a pinch.
                Come find me, she said. Baby, I know
        where you are, let's not play this game. It's too close
to the real thing.

        . . .

The old tend to take their time. Like Victor, a friend of mine who
sits reading translations of The Lawless Decade, plastic cup teetering
on the bottleneck of cool mineral water, stippled wet with beads
in 96 degree heat. Withholding, gladly, from himself.

        . . .

Come find me, said the truth
which, we are told, is out there. There are too many places
to hide. Pulling a blanket around her waist
                    Gillian Anderson revealed
in an interview of twenty relevant questions, her favorite
fruit: strawberry. And her favorite ice cream flavor: vanilla bean—
a sexual reference I now appreciate (having seen vanilla bean
seed pods in the raw).

     . . .

What's it like to be reflected?
From how many angles might it be safe to see yourself?
                              Two? Three?
And I suppose the filter will have something to say
                    about the deal. I'd give it all away to feel
familiar and safe, although I only mean that, truly, when I have
been too long lonely.
          Don't allow me to turn out that way.
                              Come find me.

     . . .

Old man Victor lifts the cup from its perch, slowly unscrews the cap
                    sits in the hiss of relief
                                   for a moment
then pours himself a fizzy inch or so, enough to empty
the neck, leaving its level at what might be called
                                        the shoulder.

ASSUMPTION

Slowly, sips.

      Ah, he says, sets it down.

           Effervescent. Small breeze, gentle
conversation at a neighboring booth.

     . . .

It's out there, she promised me

                             truth

with misty eyes, soft hips and everything I ever wanted
wrapped in tentacles of gunsmoke.

      There's not much to say about the eerie, whistling intro.
And despite my most obvious instincts, I will not make a probe joke.

      The truth is, that rumble of adolescence was nothing
more than a placeholder, the hunching Cro-Magnon in the midst
of a timeline, unfolding

            in the way that jellyfish roamed like prehistoric Darwin,
mammoth poachers of the ocean's underbelly, devouring slow and timid
soles who didn't know enough to climb up on the beach and breathe.

There's no need to search the sky for truth.
There's enough swirling ineternity. Incongruencies planted
for the sake of mystery, seeds of wonder. Exceptional bean, or pea
beneath the king's many mattresses.

                     It is enough to inspire awe.

                         Which is real.

It's enough to find joy in what it means to be: a life well lived, fleeting
almost giddy with excitement and guilt, swishing my feet, holding still
when two beady eyes appear on the horizon.

      A night spent on my belly and elbows, hypnotized
by color and mystery, and hope. My father somewhere behind me
asleep in the armchair, his tired hand gently holding the remote.

Collect

Braced with two hands on the basin
I find my eyes in the freckled mirror.
The city stoic over my shoulder, blinks.

Droplets collect in the mouth of the tap.
Brown paper package wrapped with string
sits lifeless on the bureau. Outside, black

wire tables with two empty seats.
Each subsequent seat, you decide, is less
empty than before. I decide the nature

of the writing changes with weather,
as the poet is pushed indoors. The man on the roof
is told to bang absently on concrete

with a rubber hammer. A steamroller flattens
blacktop after breakfast, beside a Christian
grammar school where a line of uniform children

hold hands down the sidewalk and stop at the light.
Parted hair, white shirts and plaid skirts billowing,
steaming sewer caps, soft heads tapped and counted.

Orchard

A boy wakes to the sound of apples
dropping into the grass (he has been sleeping
under a tree) – a bird cuts across the sky
& lands on water. The bird becomes the center
of circles expanding concentrically
from midpoint 'duck.' A silly thing to note, he admits,
as the thoughts of the newly wakened often are.
Sun jumps in white legs from the blade
he has taken from his pocket & unfolded.
The world has retreated into a pile of leaves
where a girl is tossing handfuls of orange & red
into the sky. Apples soften in pockets of their dropping.
He shaves away the bark of the tree he has been
napping against, begins to carve the sins
of his life, all he can remember
from the Sermon on the Mount, (which appears
as idea, in symbol), in deep,
hacking strokes. The duck shudders
& rises from the water, sheds rain from oiled feathers.
Lost in this fury of strokes, one serrated shadow.
The man wipes sweat from his brow
with the back of his hand, folds the blade away.
It's dark now, different bids.
He shivers in the dusk of his creation:
covered in wood shavings, surrounded by stumps.

Wicker Basket

None of this
is worth saving
until we admit that
everything is

somehow relevant: splinters
of wicker from an apple basket—
relics seem to be
enough.

Chill of winter—
apple core, crumpled
napkin on a plate—
bone white, unblinking, alive

like the gentle rushing streams
slicing through the orchard.
And the orchard. Again, the orchard.
Where what falls must be forgiven.

Notes

"Impetus" refers to French philosopher Jean Buridan and the allegory of the ass, which is, among other things, a satire of the paradox of natural balance, for he preferred his own "Theory of [internal] impetus" to theories of externally inspired momentum.

"Memorial Day": The song lyric "I'll start this off without any words" is from Nirvana's "On a Plain."

"Bad Boy" was inspired by the Eric Fischl painting of the same title.

"Fennel": Pheidippides is the ancient Greek figure who ran 150 miles in 2 days to deliver word to Athens that the Persians had been defeated in the battle of Marathon; *fennel* is the Greek word for *marathon*.

"Selene" is the Greek moon goddess, daughter of Titans.

"Anteros" is the Greek god of requited love, brother of the famed Eros (Cupid).

"Recruiting Adlai" refers to Adlai Stevenson II, 31st Governor of Illinois.

"Sunday Morning Coming Down" takes its title and sentiment from the song by Kris Kristofferson.

Acknowledgments

Thanks to my family and friends for their support, John O'Connor for his guidance and conversation, and the editors of the journals where these poems were initially published, sometimes under different titles or in slightly different forms.

After Hours
Atticus Review
Bone Orchard Review
Boston Literary Magazine
Chicago Journal of Modern Poetry
Contemporary American Voices
Danse Macabre
Decades Review
Downer Literary Magazine
Emerge Literary Journal
Eunoia Review
Hobo Camp Review
The Idiom
Indigo Rising
Ishaan Literary Review
Lascaux Review
The Legendary
The Mayo Review
Midwest Literary Magazine
Midwestern Gothic
New Plains Review
Otoliths
Poetry Quarterly
Red River Review
Rufous City Review

San Pedro River Review
The Stray Branch
Subliminal Interiors
Taj Mahal Review
Underground Voices
Wilderness House Literary Review
Willows Wept Review

"Potential" appeared in the *Poised in Flight* Anthology collected by Kind of a Hurricane Press.

Some of these poems previously appeared in the e-chapbook *Seeds* (Kind of a Hurricane Press).

Jim Davis is a graduate of Knox College. He lives, writes, and paints in Chicago, where he edits the *North Chicago Review*. His work has appeared in *Seneca Review, Adroit Journal, Blue Mesa Review, Poetry Quarterly, Whitefish Review, The Café Review*, and *Contemporary American Voices*, in addition to winning the Line Zero Poetry Contest, Eye on Life Poetry Prize, multiple Editor's Choice awards, and a recent nomination for the Best of the Net Anthology.

In addition to the arts, Jim is an international semi-professional football player.

www.jimdavispoetry.com

Praise for *ASSUMPTION*:

Davis has a wry Zen acceptance of what IS, the way the Beats did in those moments of startling wisdom. Canny, brilliant, and unerringly insightful, Jim Davis lives in a world where nothing is ordinary.

—Robin Stratton, *Boston Literary Magazine*

Jim Davis' poems are densely packed kernels of powerful language and images. They invite us to consider, as readers, some of poetry's most essential questions.

—Ian Chung, *Eunoia Review*

Jim Davis speaks Chicago's inscrutable language. Toeing the line between erudite and familiar, spliced with images only a visual artist can provide, his writing continues to deliver in the most surprising, grateful ways.

—Terri Geary, Mite Press

Other Titles by unbound CONTENT

A Strange Frenzy
By Dom Gabrielli

At Age Twenty
By Maxwell Baumbach

Before the Great Troubling
By Corey Mesler

Elegy
By Raphaela Willington

Inspiration 2 Smile
By Nate Spears

Painting Czeslawa Kwoka
By Theresa Senato Edwards and Lori Schreiner

Saltian
By Alice Shapiro

The Pomegranate Papers
By Cassie Premo Steele

and many more.

Browse our bookshelf:
unboundcontent.com

www.ingramcontent.com/pod-product-compliance
Lightning Source LLC
Chambersburg PA
CBHW051722090426
42738CB00010B/2043